PURIFY

PURIFY

WHAT CLEAN WATER TEACHES US ABOUT MAKING
SMARTER DECISIONS IN BUSINESS AND IN LIFE

RICHARD E. ALLRED

Binding Yoke Publishing

11880 North Athena Dr.

Highland, Utah 84003

www.bindingyokepublishing.com

Publisher's Cataloging-In-Publication Data

Names: Allred, Richard E., author.
Title: Purify: what clean water teaches us about making smarter decisions
    in business and in life / Richard E. Allred.
Description: [Highland, Utah] : Binding Yoke Publishing, [2019] | Includes
    bibliographical references.
Identifiers: ISBN 9781733464802 | ISBN 9781733464826 (ebook)
Subjects: LCSH: Decision making. | Leadership. | Interpersonal relations.
    | Water--Purification.
Classification: LCC HD30.23 .A45 2019 (print) | LCC HD30.23 (ebook) | DDC
    658.403--dc23

Printed in the United States of America

To all the people and organizations struggling to bring clean water to the developing world

Praise

"*Purify* gives you a greater appreciation not only for the clean water we enjoy, but also for how the process translates to cleaning up business practices. Soak up Richard Allred's terrific advice—you'll remember it every time you turn on the tap!"

—Harvey Mackay, author of the #1 New York Times best seller
Swim With The Sharks Without Being Eaten Alive

"What a great example of how our decisions influence the ripple effect of trust. *Purify* is not only a memorable title it's a great mantra for business and life."

—Stephen M. R. Covey, author of the *New York Times* best seller,
The Speed of Trust

"Water treatment expert Richard E. Allred has poured an industry's worth of wisdom into *Purify*, the must-read book for every leader, teacher, and parent who wants to set a good example, make smart decisions, and lead a happy, fulfilling life."

—Carlos Wizard Martins, entrepreneur and author of
Awaken the Millionaire Within

"*Purify* is full of refreshing new ways to help us navigate today's polarized, partisan society. Sensible, win-win, positive decision-making is a missing ingredient in much of our civil dialogue. Water treatment CEO Richard E. Allred has pooled decades of practical wisdom together with clean water industry best practices for anyone who wants to make better decisions, be more productive, and be refreshed with solutions to life's vexing challenges."

—W. Craig Zwick, Emeritus General Authority,
The Church of Jesus Christ of Latter-day Saints and Chairman,
Zwick Construction Company

Contents

Foreword

My first introduction to Richard Allred came when we moved from Minnesota to Utah. I used to play basketball at 6:00 a.m. with Richard and several other young men at the local church gym. I learned very quickly that you didn't want Richard on the opposing team guarding you because he had an unlimited amount of energy. Even when you didn't have the ball, Richard was in your face.

It has been very inspiring to sit in the front row these past thirty years and watch Richard take the same energy he exhibited on the basketball court and apply it to all areas of his life: academics, business, and, most importantly, his personal and family life.

Richard, thank you for being so real, open, raw, and vulnerable by sharing your life lessons on how to use time wisely to find more success. I have heard it said that the definition of success is duration, that anyone can get lucky once, but real success is doing something successful multiple times.

What I have learned firsthand from knowing Richard and from reading this book is that the real definition of success is not just being successful in one aspect of your life but applying the principles in this book to be successful in all aspects of your life: faith, family, friends, and financial endeavors.

This year I turned sixty. I look forward to implementing the principles Richard shares in this book to accomplish more, to prioritize what matters most, to be more balanced and successful in all aspects of my life, and to make the last third of my life the most successful, meaningful, and happy.

—Greg Butterfield, Managing Partner, SageCreek Partners

CHAPTER 1

Cleaner Water, Better Decisions

What Really Happened in Flint, Michigan?

You probably saw the headlines or caught a news report on television. Something about a federal emergency in the Detroit suburb of Flint over contaminated water. Maybe you remember the pictures and videos of the orange tap water. Undrinkable.

From 2014 to 2018, contaminated water exposed tens of thousands of Flint residents to bacteria, lead, and unsafe levels of water treatment chemicals.[1] People were poisoned by their own faucets. Hundreds packed local hospitals. At least a dozen died. Expect that toll to rise exponentially in the coming years from cancers linked to excessive amounts of those contaminants. If that weren't enough, the water was also to blame for expensive property damage to homes and businesses. The overchlorinated water destroyed engines at Flint's General Motors plant. To be fair, chlorine has saved billions of lives since London and Chicago first used it to treat public drinking water over one hundred years ago. But in water treatment, too much of a good thing is deadly.

How could a disaster like this happen in the most prosperous civilization in human history? Well, I don't want to throw you into a panic, but tragedies like Flint happen *a lot*. In the water treatment purification systems industry, headlines like "Contaminated Water Harms Local Population" and "Boil Water Order in Place" are a daily read. I've seen what happened in Flint, Michigan, take place again and again across both North and South America where my company, ATS, operates. A crisis usually goes something like this:

Local officials want to win the public's favor. Sometimes they promise to cut taxes—and they cut corners, too. One of those corners is usually water treatment. *Our water's great!* they think. *We'll just wait and see if we really need to do anything about it—rather than spend all this money on precautions.* Aging infrastructure is abandoned—cue

---

[1] "Flint Water Crisis Fast Facts," CNN, July 2, 2019, www.cnn.com/2016/03/04/us/flint-water-crisis-fast-facts/index.html.

contamination. Sometimes it's too much lead or arsenic. Other times it's a deadly bacteria. Once in a while, someone gets careless with fluoride or other treatment products. As soon as the public realizes they're poisoning their families every time they get a glass of water, the leaders responsible for the neglect play the blame game. Emotions govern every decision, and nothing gets done.

In the case of Flint, it all began when county officials approved a plan to build a new water pipeline. Sourcing water from the Flint River rather than Detroit's city water system looked smart on paper. I'm sure everyone involved congratulated themselves for saving money. Four months into the water source switch, residents complained about foul-smelling tap water. Bacteria. Officials boosted chlorine levels to kill it all. But they overlooked Flint's aging infrastructure, which let that bacteria take cover and build up in leaky valves, causing corrosion and pitting in the piping. That's when Detroit came to the rescue. They suggested that Flint abandon the new pipeline and reconnect to Detroit's more expensive (but much cleaner) water.

But Flint officials refused. Twice. The second time, a vote to reconnect *did* pass city council, but the state-appointed emergency manager overruled it. Bad decision after bad decision after bad decision. I'm sure the emergency manager felt pressured to make the new pipeline work. Regardless, that decision is going to haunt him and the one hundred thousand people of Flint for years to come. When politicians compete for higher ground, they throw maintenance (and the truth) to the wolves.

Five years later, the city did finally switch back to Detroit water so that infrastructure upgrades could be made. After a state of emergency, countless criminal investigations, a parade of political positioning, and a $97 million settlement, Flint's water is now safe. I wish other cities would learn Flint's lesson, but there's no stopping unreasonable leaders who let emotions drive decisions.

The city of Sandy, Utah, made headlines in 2019 when water treatment personnel overfluoridated the water because of faulty or inadequate feed equipment.[2] Officials didn't want to own up to their mistakes. When they drafted a warning letter to citizens, they removed a statement required by law. "Warning: Dangerous. Do Not Drink." Instead, they softened the message. "We've had a little bit of a problem with your water." In a four-block area, this "little bit of a problem" caused an estimated $3.5 million in property damage. In a few days, water heaters, plumbing, piping, and property values were destroyed. Not to mention the public's confidence in their water system. I can't imagine how costly the health effects will be in the years to come. Too much fluoride in your drinking water damages the composition of your bones and can cause other health issues. Excessive fluoride also corrodes metal, sending unsafe levels of lead and copper out through the tap.

---

[2] "'I wasn't on top of this': At Sandy Town Hall Meeting, Mayor Answers Questions about Bad Water and Lack of Communication," Nate Carlisle, *Salt Lake Tribune,* February 19, 2019, www.sltrib.com/news/politics/2019/02/19/sandy-town-hall-meeting.

I could spend the rest of this book on a "lowlights reel" of preventable water treatment disasters. Like the state of Texas, which pumped in zebra mussel-infested water from Oklahoma without treatment or control measures.[3] In Utah, the mayor of Goshen shrugged off *E. coli* in residents' water for years.[4] One state over, the Environmental Protection Agency spilled three million gallons of mine wastewater into Colorado's Animas River (and refused to compensate for damages).[5] Brazil's Brumadinho dam collapse claimed more than two hundred lives.[6] Boston's water distribution system pipe rupture took clean water away from two million people.[7] Water system contamination in Sydney, Australia, exposed three million Aussies to disease-causing parasites.[8] A Pleasant Grove, Utah, pool hospitalized fifty people due to chlorine poisoning.[9] A study that found that "safe"

---

[3] "The Zebra Mussel Threat," Texas Parks and Wildlife, accessed September 30, 2019, https://tpwd.texas.gov/huntwild/wild/species/exotic/zebramusselmap.phtml.

[4] "2 Years Later, Mandatory Boil Order Still in Place for Some Goshen Residents," Nicole Vowell, KSL.com, July 31, 2017, www.ksl.com/article/45245321/2-years-later-mandatory-boil-order-still-in-place-for-some-goshen-residents.

[5] "What the EPA Was Doing When It Sent Yellow Sludge Spilling into a Colorado Creek," Sarah Kaplan, *Washington Post,* August 10, 2015, www.washingtonpost.com/news/morning-mix/wp/2015/08/10/what-the-epa-was-doing-when-it-sent-yellow-sludge-spilling-into-a-colorado-creek/?noredirect=on.

[6] "Brumadinho Dam Collapse in Brazil: Vale Mine Chief Resigns," BBC News Service, March 3, 2019, www.bbc.com/news/business-47432134.

[7] "Ruptured Pipe Cuts Water in Boston," Derrick Henry, *New York Times,* May 3, 2010, www.nytimes.com/2010/05/03/us/03boston.html.

[8] Peter McClellan, *Sydney Water Inquiry, Fifth Report: Final Report Volume 2* (New South Wales, Australia: NSW Premier's Department, 1998).

[9] "Pleasant Grove Pool Ordered to Create New Protocol after Chlorine Incident Sent 50 to Hospital," Braley Dodson, *Daily Herald,* June 7, 2019, www.heraldextra.com/news/local/north/pleasant-grove/pleasant-grove-pool-ordered-to-create-new-protocol-after-chlorine/article_219e77c0-8888-53aa-9eaa-6283935fc8c8.html.

bottled water contains toxic microplastics.[10] In every water crisis around the world, it's the same story. Bad decisions subject the public to health risks, waste water, kill time, and often destroy lives.

What Clean Water Teaches Us about Good Decision-Making

Contaminated water is the number one killer on the planet.[11] It supersedes heart attacks, cancer, drunk driving, terrorism—everything. Find that hard to believe? Malaria alone kills more than one million people every year, and it's one of countless waterborne illnesses.[12] The bottom line is that without clean water, you die. You can't say that about much else in this world. Water treatment affects all seven and a half billion of us, and we have the capacity to get it right every time.

In water treatment, our decisions have consequences that reach farther than the tap. How many people does any given water system affect? Maybe a few hundred in a small village to thousands of people, maybe millions. My company, ATS, treated more than forty-eight trillion gallons of drinking water from 2014 to 2018. By the time I've published this book, we'll have treated hundreds of thousands of gallons in Mali,

[10] "If You Drink Bottled Water, You Could Double How Many Microplastic Particles You Ingest, Study Says," Susan Scutti, CNN, June 5, 2019, www.ksl.com/article/46567319/drinking-bottled-water-could-double-how-many-microplastic-particles-you-ingest-study-says.
[11] "World Water Day Report," World Health Organization, March 22, 2017, www.who.int/water_sanitation_health/takingcharge.html.
[12] "Malaria in Africa," Unicef, June 2018, https://data.unicef.org/topic/child-health/malaria.

Africa, 285 billion gallons in Brazil, and 142 billion in the United States during 2019.

Every decision we make at ATS affects other people. Everyone wants to drink, eat, shower, and poop! Yet most people have no idea how hard it is for clean water to come out of their taps, to make dams work, or to keep sewage out of waterways. Most of us don't know much about water treatment beyond the plot of the Julia Roberts's film *Erin Brockovich*. Most people in developed nations cannot remember a time before clean, drinkable water was available from every faucet.

Do you know how much water you use every day? Sure, you *drink* water, but you also *use* water, or water is used with everything you do. Does your car run on gasoline? Do you heat your home or office with natural gas? Own a smartphone? Oil refineries, utility companies, and computer chip manufacturers use billions of gallons of water to bring us these modern conveniences.

Do you use the internet? Water cools the technology that delivers your connection. Most data centers have huge cooling towers through which water evaporates. If they don't, then chances are they rely on hydroelectric plants for the energy to stay running. Have you ever driven by these cooling towers, seen steam rising, and thought, *Ugh, pollution?* No, it's pure water! Even the food you see on your table needed water to grow. Before you could buy a pound of almonds at the grocery, an almond grower used treated water to cover their farm thirty-eight inches deep over the course of a season. Even when you think you're conserving water at home, the agriculture that provides our food sucks up 77 percent of all clean water.

To conserve water (and time), we must take care to put smart practices and protocols in place. Engineering firms, water treatment companies like ATS, and city water plants design these practices and protocols. And it's not always a textbook solution—we learn as we go. The complexity of water chemistry makes it so that total customization is inefficient. We document everything to see what worked (and what didn't) to solve the last headline-grabbing water crisis. If a process produces results, we make it a best practice for everyone. Let's look at an example.

When ATS services a new water treatment plant, the first step is to meet with plant management to see how they operate. Every plant is different because every water source is different. Cookie-cutter approaches don't work. Some water treatment plants are blessed with clean water flowing in. Others pull water from dirty rivers or lakes. Meeting with management and observing the plant allows us to identify problems and opportunities for improvement. That said, few plant managers want to make changes unless there's a compelling reason—even if better solutions are available. That's true for everyone. We usually need a bur in our saddle to push us into action. It's all too easy to become content in our comfort zone. For this reason, when managers are open to improving, bureaucratic efforts in budgeting and purchasing can stifle the desire to embrace innovation. If we're able to prove with data that we can improve a water system, many managers will listen. This industry rewards patience. The cycle of selling new technology to a water plant is twelve to eighteen months. I tip my hat to those who quickly embrace innovation and have the political clout to force adaptation—it's rare.

In most communities and companies, a problem has to grab a leader's attention before they'll ask for help. For Flint, the trigger to act should've been the reports of foul-smelling water. In other cases, new regulations pass that demand an improvement to water quality. ATS has professional consultants who present our services to city water plants that we know could benefit from using artificial intelligence and the latest generation of chemical blends.

"Here are the improvements you can make that will give you better results," our consultants say. "Here are the problems you can solve, the risks you can reduce, and the money you can save. These are the results we've helped other cities like yours achieve. We're confident we can help yours as well."

If the water plant gives ATS the go-ahead, step one begins. We review the plant's current water treatment process. We look at how clean their water quality is in the end and how much waste sludge the process generated. We evaluate opportunities for the plant to be environmentally responsible and to maximize treatment chemicals' performance. Are they using too much chlorine for disinfection? Are they aging their equipment too fast from corrosion? What symptoms point to a problem or improvement opportunity? What capabilities are they underutilizing?

The second step is education. Although many plant managers have twenty to thirty years of experience, in many cases their knowledge is limited to their own plants. This is why third-party water treatment companies are helpful. We become their partners. We help them understand new trends, technologies, and practices that break away from outdated methods.

The third step is bench testing. Some water treatment plants can test green chemical samples on their source water, typically in jars, for free. We compare the plant's current treatment to a higher-performing alternative. Although this isn't a perfect replication of a full-scale plant pilot test, it shows us the basic differences with zero risk. Ideally, this entire process is data-driven. Testing subjected to opinion in lieu of results is disastrous. If it can't be measured, it shouldn't be used. If plant management likes what they see, we discuss a full-scale pilot test, which takes anywhere from a few weeks to a full year.

The fourth step is to present the full-scale pilot results to city officials and suggest a plan of action. Once we get started, we tweak the plan to make sure the biggest problems are solved in the safest, most efficient way possible. We treat the water generously but carefully at first to ensure the best water quality. Then we gradually back off until we've proven we can maintain that quality. Water treatment products can take anywhere from twelve to thirty-six hours to make it all the way through a water plant. We might need to change the chemistry, then wait a day and a half before we can test our change. We also have to account for residual from our previous treatments.

As you can see, nothing about water treatment is fast or easy. It's tempting to let emotions guide our decisions. To speed it up. To make educated guesses. To hope for the best. To cheat the process. Sometimes officials come right out and say to us, "Why can't you do this quicker?" Well, we can't. As CEO, I'd love to say that the jar test works perfectly every time and call it a day. After all, we don't get paid until we reach step four. But the drinking water supply is so important to the general population that we never use a quick fix. When you're dealing with water, you're dealing with human life. Better to get it done right the first time than to face the alternative. Make the right decision at every step, and we ultimately save water and time. Go with our gut or make snap judgments, and we waste both.

Only So Much Water, Only So Much Time

Decades ago, I learned about finite resources in Marketing 101. Think time, money, and natural resources. As far as we know, our planet is a closed system. A closed system is a system that doesn't allow transfers in or out. The water we have on this planet right now is all we're going to get. In that respect, water is like real estate. I'm sure you've heard real estate investors say, "Location, location, location! It's all about location!" True. Nobody is making any more real estate. And we're not making any more water. Yes, we recycle it. But when we're polluting the water, it's harder to use and more costly to treat. It's wise to conserve as much as possible.

Like water, time is also a closed system. No matter where we live, which family we were born into, or what our station in life, we all get twenty-four hours a day. You can't buy more, and you can't borrow from others.

I believe all principles are spiritual in nature, a belief that stems from my devotion to Jesus Christ and his teachings. From a religious perspective, we look at this life as a probationary period. We have a start date and an end date. You're born and you die. Everything you need to do must be accomplished between those two dates. You can lengthen your lifetime and increase your quality of life by spending time with loved ones, exercising, and eating healthy. Even so, every lifetime is a closed system. We only have so much time. And we only have so much water.

The bigger picture is this: When we make wise decisions about how we use our limited resources, we have good outcomes. When we don't, we get *Erin Brockovich*. When we are shortsighted, emotions lead us. We knowingly contaminate, thinking the consequences will never catch up to us. They *always* catch up to us. Even if we're not penalized for misusing water, it's going to cost more.

Bad decisions waste what we can't afford to lose. Because Flint built a new water pipeline without upgrading the distribution system, thousands of government officials wasted years trying to restore the original status quo—clean water. The truth is, Flint happens to all of us. Like their city officials, we let emotions, tough situations, and negative traits drive our decision-making. Then we suffer the consequences. We waste precious time reversing the bad decisions we never should have made. Exactly how much time do we waste? I recently learned the answer, and it changed everything I thought I knew about good leadership.

The 40 Percent Rule

In Brazil, where ATS treats drinking water, we have to deal with the ramifications of an unfortunate statistic every day. While I was presenting to a group of industry leaders in Rio de Janeiro at the FIRJAN Conference on Environmental Actions, I heard another presenter say that nearly 40 percent of treated water in some systems gets lost. Infrastructure leaks. People in overcrowded *favela* (slum) neighborhoods cut into the water lines or bypass their meters just to stay alive. Many depend on this pilfered water to sustain their families.

The 40 percent water statistic is tragic, infuriating, and also ironic. Why ironic? Because I learned in one of my business school textbooks that the average leader wastes 40 percent of their time undoing bad decisions. That's true whether you lead a water treatment company like ATS or a software company or a church congregation.

In my industry, wasted water means wasted time, and vice versa. Yet when we make good decisions, we save both. We all want to make good decisions. Think about that 40 percent of your day that you waste at work. That's three and a half hours each day, every day. Perhaps you start a new project. Excited to get moving, you write up a project brief. You assign every team member their tasks, and they get started. Wait! Somebody misunderstood a critical assignment. Turns out your instructions weren't as clear as you thought. You drop what you're doing and rewrite the project brief. Another employee raises their hand. Why did the brief change? How does that affect the work they've already done? Emails and calls about the two briefs keep you busy all morning. You're frustrated, tired, and hungry. It's not even noon. That one bad decision—rushing the project brief because you felt excited—ate up 40 percent of everyone's day. Sometimes you have to slow down to speed up.

The act of making a bad decision isn't what wastes time. In water treatment, most bad decisions are made in haste to find shortcuts and to save time and resources. When enough time passes and we see the outcome (not a good one), what happens? We make reversing that bad decision our top priority.

Multiply this 40 percent rule by your workday, and you lose almost eighteen hours per week. Seventy hours per month. More than thirty-six hundred hours per year! And that's just you. When a leader makes a decision, management, employees, contractors, students, or family members invest time and resources on implementation. Multiply that time wasted by the number of people who report to you. That total number should wake you up like a glass of cold water in the face.

Every time we let greed, procrastination, or even unbridled excitement guide a decision, we compromise. Compromises always come back to bite us. That wound takes a long time to heal—and that's time we won't get back. While developing processes and treatments to conserve water, I've learned a thing or two about making wise, principled decisions. Frankly, I don't feel like I've had a choice. With millions of lives on the line, I can't afford to let emotion into any of those four steps of water treatment. Cut one corner, and contaminated water could flow out of thousands of taps, spreading disease and destroying property.

I wrote this book because I believe in conserving our most precious resources. People in my industry get caught up in tangents about global warming or plastic bottles polluting our oceans. We send a message out to kids that says, "Conserve water." The message should be, "Use *all* resources wisely and conservatively. All things in moderation and temperance. Understand the root issues. Don't focus on the social media trend of the month."

This book is for people in all phases of life, from students to seasoned professionals, from new parents to chief executives. Why everybody? Because everybody who desires more from life has the same 8,760 hours in a year. *Everybody* wants to save time. And *everybody* makes decisions. The 40 percent rule touches all people, regardless of your industry, age, or faith. It doesn't matter how much money or power you have. We're all limited by the number of hours in each day. If we can almost double our productivity by making better decisions, how much further ahead would we be in our careers? In our lives?

With this book, I intend to give you 40 percent of your day back. A bold promise, I know. In the chapters ahead, I share everything I've learned about smart decision-making. All my examples come from years spent in water treatment, in service to Christ's church, and in support of my dear wife, Cara, raising and rearing our six children. These lessons from business and from life can help you make better decisions, too. When you're finished with this book, you will do the following:

- Spend more time doing what you love.

- Work smarter, not harder.

- Move up in your career or industry faster.

- Reverse bad decisions and get unstuck from their consequences.

- Stress less about deadlines so that you can meet them.

- Shoot straight with everyone in your life without worrying about what they think.

- Stop wasting time trying to figure out your mistakes.

- Make healthy food choices a habit, even if you're no fan of green smoothies.

- Invest wisely, get out of (or stay out of) debt, and leave a legacy.

- Get home to your family sooner (no more sunrise to sundown shifts).

- Choose better friends, better employees, and better clients.

- Get along with people, even if you don't see eye to eye.

- Give your employees, students, or family more predictability.

- Get more referrals to new opportunities.

- Earn trust, goodwill, and quick forgiveness if you do make a mistake.

- Save money so that you can meet financial obligations like payroll (because you no longer have people implementing and reversing poor decisions).

Good decisions influence all areas of your life at every stage. You'll be amazed how your attitudes, finances, and relationships improve when you purify your decisions with sound judgment and time-tested principles. Before you can treat water, you have to understand the chemistry of water. Before you can make good decisions with consistency, you have to understand neuroscience. What goes on in your brain before you choose the doughnut or the apple? In water treatment, we've turned wise decision-making into a science. But you don't need a science degree to make better choices with ease. All you need is a willingness to learn.

CHAPTER 2

The Neuroscience of Decision-Making

The Stench of Bad Decisions

My wife, Cara, and I have a blended family with six children. When our oldest child turned thirteen, I packed the kids into the Yukon and drove them all down to our local sewage treatment plant.

"Why are we here?" our eldest, Elle, asked when we rounded the last turn. The first treatment clarifier tank came into view. (Clarifiers are settling tanks built with mechanical means for continuous removal of solids being deposited by sedimentation. A clarifier is generally used to remove solid particulates or suspended solids from liquid for clarification or thickening.)

"You'll see," I told Elle. I pulled into the parking spot closest to the treatment clarifier, rolled down the windows, and turned the car off.

Imagine the filthiest portable toilet you've ever had the misfortune of using. Maybe it was the last day of a three-day weekend festival. Or the lone portable at a city park that parks and recreation forgot about over the summer. Remember the odor? Of course you do.

The sewage smell coming in through the car windows that day smelled ten times worse. Our kids' shrieks reverberated across the plant, followed by gagging sounds. Everybody pulled their shirts up over their noses.

"Dad! What are you doing? This is *awful*"

"Remember this smell," I said. "I've spent almost my entire adult life in water treatment, so I'm used to it. I've become desensitized. That's exactly what I do *not* want to happen to you."

"*Dad!* What are you even talking about? That's gross!"

"You're all getting to be the age where you're going to be exposed to some pretty nasty things at school, on television, and on the internet. Be careful what you listen to, what you watch, and what you look at. Whatever you let into your mind now determines the decisions you make ten, twenty, fifty years from now. Small daily decisions lead to big things down the road. Creating good patterns and success in your life starts with making lots of small, clean decisions today."

My epic dad speech continued despite the gagging. I kept the windows down. "We live within fifteen minutes of this sewage treatment facility, but we don't live right next to it. You can choose never to come here again. When you go on the internet, you can be tempted to look at things you shouldn't, but that doesn't mean you don't have a choice. You *always* have a choice. Decide what you're going to do and who you're going to be today, and you won't make a decision you'll regret later. Remember what you smelled here today. Remember that you can choose not to come back here again. You don't have to participate in filth. And remember that you *always* have a choice."

What Happens in Your Brain When You Make a Decision?

Have you ever heard someone say, "I've made up my mind"? How about, "It sounded like a good idea at the time"? Or, "I don't know why I said that; it just came out"? You've probably said things like this at some point in your life, maybe even earlier today. Statements like these let colleagues, friends, and family know how you feel about the decisions you've made. They also reveal how you made up your mind.

Like the clean water we often take for granted, most of us don't know how we make decisions. Or, to be more accurate, how *our brains* make decisions. According to the last twenty-five years of neuroscience, decision-making is more emotional than rational and more biological than logical.

Since the early 1990s, neuroscientists Antonio and Hannah Damasio have studied brain-damaged individuals to solve the mystery of human consciousness. Together, they've built one of the world's largest brain injury databases, consisting of brain injury studies and imaging test results. You might say that the Damasios know more about our brains than just about anyone.

That's why we can't shrug off their peculiar discovery about how we make decisions. One of the people they studied—Elliot[13]—underwent an operation to remove a tumor from his brain's orbitofrontal cortex[14] (OFC) just behind the eyes. It just so happens that this banana-shaped area of the brain is where we feel emotions, which allows us to make decisions, among other things. Mess with the OFC, and you mess with your ability to feel any emotion at all—or to make decisions. The surgery saved Elliot's life, but he no longer experiences emotion. Because of this impairment, he can't make even the simplest of decisions you and I don't think twice about. What should he eat for breakfast? Which route should he take to avoid heavy traffic? Should he catch up on emails first or dive right into the day's big project? Elliot can't *decide* because he can't *feel*.

We could go deeper into the science, but I don't intend for this book to be a companion to a self-study neuroscience course. If you're curious

---

[13] "Feeling Our Way to Decision," *Sydney Morning Herald,* February 28, 2009, www.smh.com.au/national/feeling-our-way-to-decision-20090227-8k8v.html.

[14] Morten L. Kringelbach, "The Human Orbitofrontal Cortex: Linking Reward to Hedonic Experience," *Nature Reviews Neuroscience* 6 (2005): 691–702, accessed September 30, 2019, www.nature.com/articles/nrn1747.

about all the ways a well-functioning OFC works, you can learn more about the Damasios' work from Antonio's TED Talk "The Quest to Understand Consciousness." But for our purposes—making better decisions—all we need to take away from Elliot's sad story is the grip our feelings have on our decisions. When we make up our minds about something, we *always* do so under the influence of emotion. If we can't feel, we can't choose. Of course, that doesn't mean we should always do as an emotion, a tough situation, or an inborn trait dictates. I'm not implying that we are or should be slaves to cravings or whim. Psychologists tell us that every decision mixes emotion and reason, but our default is to feel, *then* decide.[15] That doesn't mean good decision-making is impossible. I believe that most successful, happy people err on the side of wisdom when they make up their minds. That's how we reach the best outcomes in life, such as harmonious relationships, a fulfilling career, and a spiritual legacy.

Think about all the decisions you've made today. You've probably made rational choices, haven't you? You didn't feel pulled about your day by this feeling or that, like a buoy in a stormy sea. Your decisions today were, for the most part, grounded in reason. Weren't they? But in light of what we know about feelings affecting every decision, how could this be? Most of our decisions are made from emotions and then justified by logic.

---

[15] "Decision-Making," Psychology Today, accessed September 30, 2019, www.psychologytoday.com/us/basics/decision-making.

When chemists are first learning how to run experiments in the lab, they know what the end result should be. To pass the exam, lazy students make all sorts of mistakes until they get a passing result. All they care about is getting the right answer, even if it means botching the experiment. The end justifies the means. Or does it? Would you want a heart surgeon who's performing open heart surgery to damage other vital organs along the way? I wouldn't.

Like the cheating chemistry student and the surgeon about to lose his license, we justify a lot of our decisions based on feelings instead of on right and wrong. In Sandy, Utah, city officials knew the water was undrinkable, but they hoped fluoride levels would recede on their own. You wouldn't want a heart surgeon who hopes surgery ends well. Cara reminds me often that hope isn't a strategy. And you wouldn't want a water treatment plant manager cheating on cleanliness reports, hoping any problems sort themselves out. Whatever field we work in, we've got to stop excusing bad decisions because of "good" intentions. Easier said than done, I know. It's tricky to keep our emotions in check during important decisions because we often don't recognize their presence. And by often, I mean 95 percent of the time.[16] Yes, you read that right—the vast majority of our decisions take place unconsciously. Thank the OFC, which translates emotion into behavior without us even knowing about it.

---

[16] "The Subconscious Mind of the Consumer (and How to Reach It)," Manda Mahoney, Harvard Business School, January 13, 2003, https://hbswk.hbs.edu/item/the-subconscious-mind-of-the-consumer-and-how-to-reach-it.

Seven Seconds of Free Will

A decade after the Damasios started their database, neuroscientists from the Max Planck Institute for Human Cognitive and Brain Sciences discovered just how early our unconscious minds make those 95 percent of decisions. It's a lot earlier than you'd think.

Professor John-Dylan Haynes and his research team scanned the brains of participants tasked with a simple decision—press a button with their left hand or their right. They got no reward or benefit either way, but they were asked to remember when they decided. Haynes's team observed the brain scans and realized that they could predict what choice the participants would make. How far in advance? Seven seconds. Seven seconds before participants consciously made their decision, Haynes knew what it would be.[17]

How could a computer program predict our choices? It sounds like science fiction, but it was fairly simple. It tracked eye movements. Push the button with your left hand, and the scan looks one way. Push with your right, the scan looks another. *Nature Neuroscience* reported Haynes's findings:

Many processes in the brain occur automatically and without involvement of our consciousness. This prevents our mind from being overloaded by simple routine tasks. But when it comes to

---

[17] "Brain Makes Decisions before You Even Know It," Kerri Smith, *Nature,* April 11, 2008, www.nature.com/news/2008/080411/full/news.2008.751.html.

decisions we tend to assume they are made by our conscious mind. This is questioned by our current findings.[18]

Some of these "many processes" are due to our genetics. Recent research links your genes to your decisions.[19] Not simple decisions like what to wear or what to eat. Genes influence complex social behavior, such as assessing risks and feeling motivated. Do these studies suggest our agency is an illusion? Does fate determine our decisions? Far from it. Our free will is more important than we realize. Haynes concludes his team's findings:

> Our study shows that decisions are unconsciously prepared much longer ahead than previously thought. But we do not know yet where the final decision is made.[20]

Let's recap this brief neuroscience lesson. Influenced by genetics and feelings, our brain makes a decision. Then we become aware of it. Then we make a "final decision" to follow through (or not). So where is the final decision made? And when? Like I told our kids, the good small and simple decisions we make today yield great things tomorrow. If 95 percent of our decisions arise from the unconscious mind, we have to wonder what's going on in there! After all, decision-making is inescapable—each of us

---

[18] Chun Siong Soon, Marcel Brass, Hans-Jochen Heinze, and John-Dylan Haynes, "Unconscious Determinants of Free Decisions in the Human Brain," *Nature Neuroscience* 11 (2008): 543–45, accessed September 30, 2019, https://www.nature.com/articles/nn.2112.

[19] "Your Genes Affect Your Betting Behavior," Robert Sanders, Berkeley News, June 16, 2014, https://news.berkeley.edu/2014/06/16/your-genes-affect-your-betting-behavior.

[20] "Unconscious Decisions in the Brain," Max-Planck-Gesellschaft, April 14, 2008, www.mpg.de/research/unconscious-decisions-in-the-brain.

makes thirty-five thousand decisions per day.[21] How do we improve the small and simple decisions we don't even realize we're making? Science gives us an answer for that, too.

Garbage in, Garbage Out

For decades, parents have known that popular music, movies, and television shows steer young people's emotions and behavior. If song lyrics praise rebellion, violence, and drug use, kids listening tend to disobey their parents, act out, and use drugs.[22] Adolescents are more impressionable than adults, but we can never outgrow natural law—you get out whatever you put in. What's true about human nature is true about nature itself. Let contaminants leak into the water supply, and you're going to make people sick. If you treat that water, you protect the public's health. In the same way, what you see, hear, or put up with becomes part of your unconscious "reservoir" that, in part, determines your choices. Remember that small and simple decisions lead to great things. "Decision-making can be seen as the link between memory of the past and future actions," recent research confirms.[23] Of course, religious believers through time knew this before science did. The gospel according to Saint Matthew (12:35), almost two thousand years old, tells humankind, "A

---

[21] "How Many Decisions Do We Make Each Day?," Eva M. Krockow, Psychology Today, September 27, 2018, www.psychologytoday.com/us/blog/stretching-theory/201809/how-many-decisions-do-we-make-each-day.

[22] Council on Communications and Media, "Impact of Music, Music Lyrics, and Music Videos on Children and Youth," *Pediatrics* 124, no. 5 (2009), accessed September 30, 2019, https://pediatrics.aappublications.org/content/124/5/1488.

[23] Lesley K. Fellows, "The Neuroscience of Human Decision-Making through the Lens of Learning and Memory," *Current Topics in Behavioral Neuroscience* 37 (2018): 231–51.

good man out of the good treasure of the heart bringeth forth good things: and an evil man out of the evil treasure bringeth forth evil things."

Fill your head with clickbait news, deceptive headlines, and social media outrage today, and tomorrow you're going to see the world in a skewed negative and all to often false way. Then it becomes likely that you'll end up making decisions you regret. Let yourself get stuck in compromising situations, and you'll compromise. Give into what feels right, and your decision won't be. What dominates our thoughts determines our decisions. Negative input, negative output. And worse, these poor choices will come naturally. The 95 percent of decisions your brain makes without you knowing about them won't be honorable, noble, or in your best interests if you feed on a constant diet of negative input.

Once pollutants enter a waterway, the likelihood of that water cleaning itself up and becoming usable again is slim. It's the same as letting negative emotions like fear or greed swirl around in your head, unchecked. Because there is no such thing as a one-time decision. Excuses like "But I'll only ever do this once" destroy public trust, bankrupt businesses, and send people to prison.

Intelligence alone cannot treat mental contaminants. Many high-IQ high-achievers make headlines for bad decisions. Remember Elon Musk's ill-advised tweet announcing he'd secured financing for Tesla? Illegal and unwise. Despite his high intelligence, Elon is just as able to make poor choices. How many accidental overdoses have claimed the lives of the outwardly successful? We've lost count by now. The same goes for athletes who lose their fortunes, celebrities who drive away loved ones, and politicians who abuse the public's trust. It's not hard to find a dozen examples of each in a few minutes on Google. In fact, psychologist Robert Sternberg believes that smart people are prone to poor decisions because they trust their intuition and its unconscious biases.[24] Intelligent people tend to be overconfident in their decisions because they've been successful before.

In a strange twist, Sternberg himself resigned as editor of a prestigious psychology journal. Colleagues forced Sternberg to apologize for the "questionable ethical practice" of citing his own work rather than citing other researchers.[25]

My point? The decision-making process is neutral. Smarts don't matter. You can get great things out of small, simple decisions you made a long time ago. To get clean water, we first have to know what contaminants are in it so that we know how to treat it. Luckily for us, wise engineers in the waterworks space figured out years ago how to treat water. They've made reservoirs. Built dams. Put in transmission lines. Identified contaminants. Designed the treatment plants and process. Then treated the water appropriately.

Just as the right water treatment makes a tank of steaming sewage clean again, it is possible to purify your mind and to make good

---

[24] "Are You Too Smart to Think Wisely?," Eva M. Krockow, Psychology Today, March 6, 2019, www.psychologytoday.com/us/blog/stretching-theory/201903/are-you-too-smart-think-wisely.

[25] "Revolt over an Editor," Colleen Flaherty, Inside Higher Ed, April 30, 2018, www.insidehighered.com/news/2018/04/30/prominent-psychologist-resigns-journal-editor-over-allegations-over-self-citation.

decisions come naturally, improving your life, your health, and your odds of success. For example, a recent study found that if you read, watch, or listen to a positive, uplifting news story, you believe there is good in the world.[26] That belief becomes part of your brain's decision reservoir, so you make choices in alignment with it. You begin to *truly believe* that the world is good! Another study traded the news for movies.[27] Participants watched films in which ordinary people took extraordinary action, self-sacrificing to save the day. Guess what effect these movies had? People came away more generous to strangers and more loyal to loved ones. Goodness in, goodness out.

Our unconscious mind drives our decisions, but we get to choose what goes into our subconscious. Learning to make good, small decisions today will bring about success down the road. We can "clean up" our mind by removing what contaminates our decisions upstream. What are those contaminants? What emotions, situations, and traits drive most bad decisions, even if we're not aware of them? Look closely enough, and everyone will find contaminants in their decision-making. We all could do better. Otherwise, you wouldn't need this book. If water was always clean, we wouldn't need water treatment.

Let's find out what's in the water.

---

[26] Karl Aquino, Brent McFerran, and Marjorie Laven, "Moral Identity and the Experience of Moral Elevation in Response to Acts of Uncommon Goodness," *Journal of Personality and Social Psychology* 100, no. 4 (2011): 703–18.

[27] Mary Beth Oliver, Tilo Hartmann, and Julia K. Woolley, "Elevation in Response to Entertainment Portrayals of Moral Virtue," *Human Communication Research* 38, no. 3 (2012): 360–78.

CHAPTER 3

Why We Make Bad Decisions

How Do You Get Clean Water?

Let's recap. First, identify what's in the water, and find the root cause of the problem. Second, treat any contaminants with the right chemistry and equipment. Third, pump the water into homes and businesses across the city's well-maintained distribution system.

All right, it's not quite that simple. The point is, we can't declare water safe until we identify and treat any chemicals, minerals, organic compounds, and microorganisms in the water. Only a reckless water treatment engineer would dump fluoride, chlorine, and other chemicals into a stream and call it a day. In this business, we must first answer the question: How *much* of each treatment chemical do we need?

I apply this logic to decisions I make every day at work, at home, and everywhere else. I don't think I can help it. I once heard someone say, "How you do *anything* is how you do *everything.*" In water treatment, I look for contaminants that cause property damage and disease. In life, I've identified contaminants that make wise decisions difficult (if not impossible)—negative emotions, compromising situations, and unproductive traits. What do I mean by emotion, situation, and trait? Let's ask the dictionary.

Emotion: a state of feeling[28]

Situation: a relative position or combination of circumstances at a certain moment[29]

Trait: a distinguishing quality of personal character[30]

Whenever we're governed by a negative emotion—for instance, fear—we cloud our judgment. We can't think smart, see straight, or act right. It can also cause us to not take action. For example, if creditors start calling, most people avoid them and hide instead of working out

---

[28] "Emotion," *Merriam-Webster Dictionary,* accessed September 30, 2019, www.merriam-webster.com/dictionary/emotion.

[29] "Situation," *Merriam-Webster Dictionary,* accessed September 30, 2019, www.merriam-webster.com/dictionary/situation.

[30] "Trait," *Merriam-Webster Dictionary,* accessed September 30, 2019, www.merriam-webster.com/dictionary/trait.

a reasonable payment plan. Over the course of a single day, negative emotions pressure us into a decision we come to regret. Ever received a tight deadline you knew you couldn't meet? The negative emotions likely cause at least one poor decision to follow. Even if we check our emotions and step back from a tough situation, an unproductive trait can take us down the wrong path. They keep us focusing on the wrong thing. Perhaps you've fought a natural inclination to procrastinate. You knew the right decision to make, and you had the ability, but you somehow kept putting it off.

For every contaminant, there's a treatment. Let's start our decision-making purification process with a study of how the three types of contaminants show up in our decisions.

What Contaminates Our Decisions?

The First Contaminant—Negative Emotions

Fear

Everybody's been afraid of failure at some point in their lives. Fear of failing a test, fear of losing a job, fear of being rejected by a loved one. Failure is uncomfortable. If that wasn't enough, we often feel like everyone expects us to explain *why* we failed. All the sordid details included.

But what I see more often (yet hear discussed much less) is the fear of success. The fear of success causes you to make decisions that lead to mediocrity. You pull back from opportunity and guard the status quo. Usually fear of success gets stirred up when you see the finish line of a task or project. Whatever victory looks like for you, it's bigger, scarier, and more complex than you imagined.

You might be thinking, *But what is there to fear about success?* At a recent tech conference, I heard a panel of entrepreneurs call out this fear.

"If I'm successful, what's next?" One entrepreneur shared his inner dialogue before cashing out of his latest software company. "Am I really going to do this? Do I really *want* to do it? What if the big payday isn't everything I dreamed it would be?"

I don't expect everyone reading this book to be a few days away from a billion-dollar exit from a business they started. What we define as success is different for everyone, but our *fear* of the what-ifs of that success are the same. I once met a gentleman who finished writing a book he never intended to publish. "I finally finished my book," he said. "But there's no way in heck I'm going to let anybody read it!" He was afraid of success and what would happen if he exposed his thoughts. What would people say? Countless musicians compose music or sing songs that the world will never hear because they're afraid to let their light shine.

Have you ever blown up an inflatable inner tube, perhaps before heading to the beach? When you first started pumping, you thought, *This is never going to fill up. I shouldn't even bother. Forget about it and get some sun.* But you kept at it, and as you got closer to fully inflating the tube, it got harder and harder to pump. As we get nearer to success, we get to a point where it becomes overwhelming because we're so close.

Greed

Most businesses don't survive past year ten. Very few make it to $10 million in annual revenue. Greed is often the culprit. Often the founder of the company tries to make sure *they* succeed at the expense of everybody else around them. Many leaders can't stomach the fact that they're paying their executive team more than they've taken home in years. So they start looking for reasons to get rid of people—the very people they need to succeed. They fire a veteran executive the first chance they get. Or they change the company compensation plan that drove success. Sooner or later, their greed drives the business into the ground.

The allure of commissions can lead other people in a company astray from sound decision-making. Salespeople in general are already good at selling. After all, they sold themselves well enough to get the job. The first day at work, they figure out how the commission structure works to make the most they can. If a sale isn't right for the company or the client, they may push to get them to go for it anyway. Sales managers have to be skilled to align compensation with desired outcomes. In water treatment, for example, we sometimes feel tempted to sell more chemical than a plant needs because we make more money. The real goal should be optimization. Use as little chemistry as possible to clean the water. Through the years, I've crossed paths with many salespeople who "bump up the pump." That's where they turn up a chemical feed pump ever so slightly that it goes unnoticed. Over time, it increases chemical consumption and therefore cost. With chemistry, more is not always better. It's often detrimental. The salesperson may get that sale, but they're wasting chemicals and water and might be damaging the system. It's natural to look out for yourself, but greed turns self-preservation into wasteful, harmful decisions.

I met an investor recently who told me how taking your company public causes a whole slew of problems. To qualify for bonuses at their now-public company, management has to meet targets that aren't in the best interests of the company. The principled decisions that made the private company successful now have to be given up. New executives take a great company and strip it down so that shareholders can look at nice short-term results. A structure built on greed incentivizes shortsighted decisions. Greedy leaders now care about getting their bonuses, retaining their jobs, and looking good to investors. Greed only works in the short term or if you don't care about sustainable success or future happiness.

In 2011, I let greed take over, and it cost me. At the time I owned a beverage company, and we'd just landed our second retail account in Japan. Our customer was recovering from the one-two punch of the earthquake and tsunami, so we were eager to help them start their business back up. We completed several transactions for them. Over the summer, their sales diminished, but they didn't report the decline to us. Then I got a message from them that I couldn't say no to. "We're placing an order four times the size of our last one, and we have to have the shipment here by the first of the month. We don't have time for you to wait for our payment to clear [international payments take up to five days to clear the bank]. Please ship our order today, and we'll pay you as soon as we receive it." Shipping first, collecting later wasn't unusual for orders within the US. But I knew better than to do this on an international transaction. I did it anyway. The promised payment would've been the biggest single check I'd ever deposited in my life at that point. So we shipped. Once products leave the shores of your country, if you don't have cash or a letter of credit, it's hard to collect if the client chooses not to pay.

Long story short, they took advantage of us. The order arrived, but our check did not. I don't think they ever planned to pay us. We hired two US-based attorneys and another in Japan. I should have pushed back and gotten paid up front, then shipped the product. We did get reimbursed but at a discounted rate, so by the time we paid our attorneys and covered the cost of lost goods, we netted zero. Sometimes you make mistakes in business and justice doesn't prevail. When that happens, it's usually because the money was too good to be true!

It's typical for small business owners to jump and say, "Yes, we can do that!" to control greed. The chairman of our board at ATS told me to have the executive team sign off on big contracts *before* we close them. The team asks, "Does this make sense for the company?" Just because an opportunity has a lot of zeros behind it doesn't mean it's the right decision for you or for the company.

When we feed greed, we feed entitlement. A few years back, an ATS chemical sales rep came up with an idea for a new treatment product. The process was a breakthrough, and everyone in the company knew it. Prior to employment, ATS employees sign a document stating that any intellectual property (IP) they develop while employed at ATS belongs to

ATS. But I felt like I ought to reward the sales rep. So I offered to pay him a royalty from every sale.

The rep countered my offer. "That's not good enough," he said. "I'm certain my idea is worth a billion dollars. I won't accept any less."

"And I thought my first offer was above and beyond." I chuckled.

"No less than one billion dollars, Rich," he said. Employees know I go by Richard.

We didn't meet his demand, and the sales rep quit a few days later. He went unemployed for many months. I heard from a mutual contact in the industry that he finally got a job . . . in a different state. His wife and kids stayed home. He drove back to see them on weekends. That's no life. All because he was sure he deserved a billion dollars for his "idea" IP that was undeveloped IP at best. That billion-dollar idea still hasn't generated any money, but ideas never do. It takes a lot of work to monetize any idea of value as well as grit to execute a plan.

Give greed an inch, and it takes a thousand miles. I once helped a friend buy out his brother from the company they started together. Against my advice, he offered his brother an amount worth more than seven times his brother's share of ownership. Even working long overtime hours, it would take ten years to earn that money back. But still, my friend's brother wasn't satisfied. Greed took hold of him and turned their sour deal into a family tragedy.

"You're taking advantage of me and trying to push me out," said the brother who'd been overpaid. "My share is worth one hundred times what you paid me."

The brothers haven't spoken since. Nor have their spouses or children. The guy got the sweetest payout I've ever seen, but greed made him a fool and ruined his relationship with his family. Entrepreneurs who work forty years never see a payout like his. Yet entitlement made him upset because he thought he deserved more.

Pride

The type of work and skill set required for building a company are completely different from those needed to optimise a large established company. I've noticed that job applicants who come from large corporations care more about power plays and empire building than steady leadership. The bureaucracy they worked within let them build silos. They isolated themselves from other leaders, departments, and teams. It's our nature to want to be in charge of our lives and to control our fate. But let that desire get out of hand, and your pride becomes your downfall.

When chatting with potential hires, I've gotten laughed at once or twice. "You want *me* to leave software to come and work in jeans with you water treatment guys?" We don't get into this business because of pride or to be flashy. Many are quiet, wear jeans, and are unassuming. Most don't worry too much about how they are seen.

Too many people make career decisions based on how they want people to perceive them. They put themselves in a position they don't enjoy. Being in a job to satisfy a need for status will make anyone miserable after a while.

Shame

You know the feeling you get when you compromise your principles . . . and you knew better? That's shame. Shame is the painful feeling after we do something dishonorable, improper, or ridiculous. It's so powerful that we want out of it no matter the cost.

Often a bad decision makes us feel guilt and shame, and another bad decision keeps us stuck in shame. How? We feel ashamed over a bad decision, so we make more bad decisions. Rather than bring it into the light, get the help we need, and fix it, we do whatever we can to cover up the mistake.

Shame dictates bad transactions all the time in mergers and acquisitions. A CEO gets excited about buying out a company. After money changes hands, he realizes it's a mistake. Some executives own up to the bad buy, sell off the new company's assets, and recoup some of what they paid. Too often CEOs let shame dictate their next moves. When the new company loses money, they pretend that everything is fine. They hope something comes along to fix it. A third-party investor. A multibillion-dollar government contract. Yet this rarely happens.

We saw this scenario play out when General Electric (GE) bought water treatment company BetzDearborn (renamed GE Betz) in 2002 for $1.8 billion.[31] Rumor in the industry had it that GE Betz underperformed from day one. Nobody thought to fix the mistake right away. The result? GE corporate played around with water treatment for fifteen years and

---

[31] "GE Entering Water Treatment Field," Dana Ambrosini, WaterIndustry.org, February 13, 2002, www.waterindustry.org/NewProjects/GE-1.htm.

didn't make the money they expected. At least they sold GE Betz for more than they paid—$3.4 billion.[32] When you account for inflation, GE made only $1 billion from the sale. That may seem like a lot of money, but when you run a company as big as General Electric, it's a real disappointment. Other investments paid out much more over the same time period.

I suspect GE Betz leaders felt ashamed over the company's poor performance. Shame doesn't pay. Best to make the right call the first time. If you don't get it right from the outset, better to make the decision shame tempts you not to make. Let shame guide you from here on out, and you'll be stuck in the cycle of shame indefinitely.

Instant Gratification

Believe it or not, infomercials work. Some people hear "Buy one knife set, get one free" at two o'clock in the morning and can't resist the "once in a lifetime opportunity." When instant gratification guides us, we run up credit card debt, get stuck in dysfunctional relationships, and hire employees who sabotage projects and our team's efforts.

Thousands of people join multilevel marketing companies (MLMs) every month. All driven by instant gratification. Years ago I met a multilevel marketer. I knew he was trying to make a living like I was, so I didn't take offense when he pitched me. The guy came by my house in a decked-out motorhome. He sold me hard—the money, the

---

[32] "SUEZ Finalizes the Acquisition of GE Water & Process Technologies," Suez.com (press release), October 2, 2017, www.suez.com/en/News/Press-Releases/SUEZ-finalizes-the-acquisition-of-GE-Water-and-Process-Technologies.

lifestyle, the status. It could all be mine if I joined. He showed me commission checks and talked about extravagant trips for top sellers.

"Let me tell you something about this MLM," he said. "My upline says that the person who is going to make the most in this MLM hasn't even joined yet. More and more people are getting in on this great opportunity every day. The sooner you join, the sooner you make money. Who knows? If you get started with me, maybe *you'll* break the company record! Are you in?"

I definitely was not. This gentleman didn't understand the first thing about pyramid schemes. You can't enter at the bottom and make good money. Everything flows upward. Someone smarter than him probably sold him on an outlandish dream, and he was desperate enough to take it. Instant gratification never leads to wealth, health, or happiness.

The Second Contaminant—Compromising Situations

Subjective Experience

"Subjective experience is not a reliable indicator of judgment accuracy," a study on decision-making reported.[33] What does that imply? That we should strategically forget the past. Just because our gut instinct was right last time doesn't mean it's right next time (or any other).

Many entrepreneurs, artists, and entertainers are one-hit wonders. That first successful start-up, album, or movie gives them *over*confidence.

---

[33] Daniel Kahneman and Gary Klein, "Conditions for Intuitive Expertise: A Failure to Disagree," *American Psychologist* 64, no. 6 (2009): 515–26.

So what happens? They make money, lose it, and can't figure out why. What worked once for you in one situation isn't repeatable unless it was principle based. History does not, in fact, repeat itself. How can it? People change. Motivations change. Technology changes. When will the exact situation where you first succeeded ever reappear in life? It won't. It can't because time doesn't work like that.

Several years ago, ATS dove into a deal to help a well-known semiconductor manufacturing company upgrade their cooling systems. (Semiconductors are used in microprocessor chips and transistors, which make computers, cell phones, and other electronics work.) As soon as we signed a contract with the manufacturer, the relationship soured. Unproductive meetings. Project micromanagement. One-size-fits-all decision-making. Company leadership approached everything the same way. How they built the world's best semiconductors was how they did payroll, finances, and maintenance. Success didn't translate. You may need months of preparation to produce a chip, but you shouldn't take weeks to decide who takes out the garbage. It was fascinating to watch how much money, time, and knowledge they wasted on simple things. Putting a bag of salt into a water softener required nine people to hold a meeting and sign off. A two-hour meeting for a two-dollar bag of salt. How easily they could double or triple their profits!

I see the same track-record mistake in water treatment. Rookie salespeople get lucky with their first sale and repeat the closing pitch word for word to the next client. If they didn't need to stick to the script and ask the first client follow-up questions, they won't with prospect number two, or so they believe. These young salespeople are still learning the science of dealmaking and the skill of a strong close. Water constituents and the necessary treatment can vary as much as the person in charge of the plant.

A situation you think you've seen before can make any sale fall through. When water treatment engineers have déjà vu, the stakes are always higher. It happens often. Veteran engineers go off previous experience, attack a new problem the same way they did the last one, and skip the lab work. It's easy to say, "I'm seeing deposits, so let's turn up the chemicals." Too much of the right chemical causes corrosion or other undesirable effects.

At the time of this writing, ATS engineers are running tests for a new client. Their problem may be with incoming water, but it could also be a powder coating on some of their water tanks. We don't know yet. So what do we tell the customer? Nothing, except to reiterate the timeline, which helps manage their expectations. Because we don't *know* anything yet. We could make a judgment call based on what we've seen in the past, but no two situations are ever alike. Until we get the test results, we can't draw conclusions. In the Google age of instant answers, nobody wants to wait. We need to anyway. Some things can be learned or understood only with real effort and persistence. The truth is worth the wait. Otherwise, we might end up with Sandy's property damage, Austin's mussels infestations, or worse.

Too Many Decisions

The more decisions you have to make at any given time, the more likely you are to make a bad one. That's according to one recent study, which had participants deciding to buy a product or join a college course. "Making choices led to reduced self-control." Their self-control depleted, participants had "less physical stamina" and "reduced persistence in the face of failure."[34] In other words, making a lot of decisions without taking time to rest wears you down and makes you compromise your values.

My father used to say, "There is never enough time to do the job right but always enough time to do it over." I've seen that play out so many times in life and in business. ATS recently took on a water cooling system project that involved just under a $1 million up-front investment. To give the client what they wanted, we had to design the systems, hire seven vendors to help, and deliver the systems to the client within four weeks.

Can we do it in this short period of time? I asked myself. Wrong question. I should've asked, *Can we do it* right *in this short period of time? Should we even do it at all?*

We entrepreneurs think we can do everything at once, but should we? No, but I didn't let that stop me. I was blinded by the promise of quick revenue. The shortened timeline meant our vendors skipped critical tests to confirm that the systems operated correctly before they

---

[34] Kathleen D. Vohs, Roy F. Baumeister, Brandon J. Schmeichel, Jean M. Twenge, Noelle M. Nelson, and Dianne M. Tice, "Making Choices Impairs Subsequent Self-Control: A Limited-Resource Account of Decision Making, Self-Regulation, and Active Initiative," *Motivation Science* 1 (2014): 19–41.

were delivered. They did not. Employees and contractors worked into the evenings and on weekends. So much had to be done so fast that I didn't think to double check our numbers. In our haste, it turns out that it cost double the amount to build the cooling trailer our client wanted. When I realized the misunderstanding, I should've talked to my CFO about getting us better terms with the client to rent out the remaining systems. I didn't. I had too much to think about to make the right decision about anything.

ATS has more opportunities than we can pursue. That cooling system deal was not the best use of company manpower and resources. I knew better—I learned about opportunity cost in Business 101. What does it cost you to go after an opportunity now instead of waiting for the next one? Failing to think that through cost me the equivalent of a few Harvard educations. I made the decision to take on the project on the fly. I was so excited for the new business that I jumped the gun. The only good decision I made during that project was to follow through on our commitment to finish the job. We took care of our client, and we delivered what they paid for on time.

I should have slowed down during that project. Now that I've learned from that mistake, I can make sure it never happens again. How? In the future, I'm going to ensure that we have realistic time frames so that we can underpromise and overdeliver. We've also set up a quality control system so that we can test every product ourselves. No more relying on manufacturers that are under extreme pressure. And above all, we're going to take things slow. If we don't take our sweet time vetting a project, we're going to lose sweet money again.

Pressure

Have you ever seen a movie where the characters execute perfect life-or-death decisions on the fly? In reality, the right decision is "Let's sleep on it," "Let's give it some time," or "Let's try four or five different ways and see what happens." Most of the time when you feel pressured into a quick decision, it's probably the wrong one.

Remember the last time you were shopping for a new car, and the salesperson offered a deal that was good "for today only"? Any good salesperson knows how to create artificial urgency. "If you don't do this now, you'll have missed your only chance!" If marketing messages or salespeople artificially pressure you to buy something, you'll regret it. Almost every time I've hired somebody or signed a contract because I felt urgency, I wished I hadn't.

Years ago, not long after I started my beverage company, I entertained a sales pitch from a marketing firm. The marketer promised us global retail presence and prime shelf space. His monthly retainer fee? A "reasonable" $20,000.

"We're in talks with three other beverage companies like yours," he told me. "The first to work with us becomes an exclusive industry partner. I worry that if you put this off for even a week, you'll lose your chance. We'll get someone else all the publicity that could've been yours."

The pressure got to me, but I didn't sign the contract he slid across the table. I wanted feedback from someone I respected. I called one of my mentors—a successful businessman whose air fresheners hang in millions of cars around the world. He suggested we all meet together at his office—me, my mentor, and this marketing guy's team.

We met the following morning.

"I'd like to introduce you to my marketing team," I said to my mentor as we all shook hands. "Well, not *officially* yet, but that's why we're here."

"Absolutely," the marketer said. "With the right marketing efforts, Richard's company can rocket to household-name status!"

"I see." My mentor nodded. "Let's go talk in my office." He motioned for me—only me—to follow. "Would you excuse us?"

"Sorry, just a minute," I said to the marketers. "Why don't you make yourselves comfortable here?"

We walked into my mentor's office together. He sat back in his leather chair and sipped some water.

"So . . ." I broke the silence.

"Yes?"

"What did you want to talk to me about privately?"

"Nothing they need to hear."

"What do you mean?" I started to sit up. "Aren't we going back out there?"

"No, they'll leave eventually."

I was stunned.

"Isn't that, you know, *rude*?"

"No, Richard. What's rude is pressuring someone into a purchase that doesn't benefit him because you have mortgage payments to make. I don't want you to get taken. People like me don't get where we are today because we paid twenty thousand a month to somebody promising the world."

I nodded. We waited and discussed family. The potential marketers left.

Keeping a level head helps you let off the pressure when no one else will. Soon after I purchased ATS from my father, we landed a water treatment contract as the prime contractor at a local military base. The deal more than doubled our revenue. The base commander and engineers wanted to minimize the amount of chemicals used to keep aircraft up and running while reducing costs. The previous contractor convinced the base commander that the new ATS technology would be better for the military and for the environment.

Once everyone signed on the dotted lines, ATS placed an order with our usual equipment supplier. We expected the complex water system installation to take six months. About four months into the process, our supplier started sending cryptic responses to our emails. Yes-or-no questions got long-winded answers we couldn't decipher. I followed up via email and phone for a while, but progress was unusually slow. My father suggested that I fly out to their headquarters in Wisconsin to see what was going on.

I called to schedule a meeting, but they kept putting me off. For a month. "We want to make sure we have everything ready to show you when you get here," they said. Fair enough. So I waited. Finally, a meeting was scheduled for mid-June, and I booked my flight.

I remember driving my rental car from the airport through cornfields to their location with the windows down. *This is a wonderful time of year to be here,* I thought.

When I got to the reception desk, a sign welcomed me. But no receptionist. There were a couple of people hanging out in the lobby.

"Hi, there," a tall man said to me. "Can we help you with something?"

"I have a ten o'clock meeting scheduled," I told him. Before I could ask if he worked at the company, one of the other men spoke.

"Great! We'll give you a tour of the facility first."

OK, strange.

"Sure," I replied. I felt like I was missing something, but both men looked confident enough.

As we walked past the employees and the manager's office, I knew something was going on. Everyone on the plant floor looked panicked with fear. Even the shift manager. I saw a group of employees speaking to each other in hushes. Maybe someone up top threatened everyone. *Here's what you can say, here's what you can't . . . or else.*

When I met the plant manager, I asked him about the status of our order. My tour guides answered me instead. I decided it was time to be blunt.

"I'm sorry, what's your position here?" I asked.

"We work with an investment firm. We've purchased this company."

"They made us an offer," mumbled the plant manager. "They're helping us get back on track."

But these finance guys have zero understanding of water treatment technology, I thought. *Or the parts we need to finish the project!*

I'm sure these investors were wonderful people, as were our supplier's employees. That was no excuse for what I saw next. The equipment we'd ordered—welding frames and membrane tubes— showed about three days' worth of work. Nowhere close to the four months of progress I'd expected. Definitely not close to the work that should have been done based on the progress payments they'd received from us.

"I can assure you, everything is in order," one of the investors told me.

"We need to talk. In private," I said. No need to berate the employees for something that clearly wasn't their doing.

The next day, I met with the investors at their office across town. It took half a day to squeeze out the truth about the real reason for the buyout—no credit, no cash, and no plans to fix it. Even worse, our down payment to secure our equipment had been used to cover rent and salaries.

"We had no choice but to take our profit up front," the other investor told me. "I'm sure you understand."

"I really don't. Where does that leave us?" I said. "ATS has to get this project done because we're under contract to do it. We sold the base commander on equipment we've ordered from this plant. I've personally committed to the base commander that we can do this, and we *will* do this. We've spent years building our reputation, and if we don't make good on this, we can destroy it. People remember bad decisions, and the military has a great memory. If we don't come through, this project will haunt us forever."

"Would you like to make an offer? To purchase our ownership stake in the supplier?"

"No, I wouldn't be interested in that," I said. "Not knowing what their financial conditions are. What about a creative solution?"

"Such as?"

"Well, we need the equipment to finish the project. I don't want to give them more money and hope they use it right. What if ATS paid *their* vendors directly? And covered all expenses related to finishing this project? That way we're funding what we need instead of funding the supplier's whole operation."

"That—" The investor glanced at his partner, who nodded. "That could work."

And it did. We made an agreement, got the supplier's CEO on board, and moved the project forward. We took over the supplier's accounts payable for the parts they bought for us, and ATS paid the invoice. We also compensated the supplier for employee labor that went into engineering the equipment. This arrangement kept our supplier in business long enough to finish the project for us. Without that agreement, I don't know that we ever would have finished the project. The pressure was on, and we came through together.

A decade earlier, we worked as a subcontractor for a large engineering firm on the same military base—similar water system, different contract.

At that time a Department of Defense executive called a status report meeting. The primary contractor's contract manager flew out from Washington, DC, and he invited me to tag along.

"We have an emergency with our water system," the base commander announced. "We expect you to have it fixed tomorrow."

Our contract doesn't stipulate a twenty-four hour response, I thought.

The prime contractor's manager stayed calm. He asked a series of questions about the problem, which the commander answered. Then the manager looked the base commander dead in the eye and said calmly, "All right, thank you for all the information. We'll take it into consideration, and we'll get you an answer in two weeks. We'll take this problem back to our office, study it, and come up with a real solution for you."

So, the customer's always right . . . until they're wrong?

"They're expecting an answer tomorrow, and you told them to wait two weeks," I said to the contract manager on our walk back to the parking lot.

"When we set this contract up, we set it up to allow us time. This is their emergency, not ours. Their failure to plan, not ours. They agreed to our contract, no matter what they say now."

The pushback ultimately led to more contracts and more profits for everyone on a better solution for the air force base. I can't imagine the consequences if we'd let the base commander pressure us. Well, I can, but they're not good. A recent study found that "the time it takes to get an answer correlates with the perceived difficulty of the decision."[35] In English now—the tighter your deadline, the riskier your decision. High-pressure decisions rarely end well. So don't attempt to make them. Stay calm. Push back. Soon I'll teach you how.

Excess

My father-in-law once told me, "If money can solve your problem, you don't have a problem. If you don't have money, great! Now you can figure out a solution."

If you don't have things operating well, more money won't fix your problem. Money can't fix bad thinking or bad processes. More money just hides your real issues. Companies do this all the time. Their cash flow is great, but then they screw things up. I see many young entrepreneurs seeking venture capital. Not because they need it but because they have problems to hide. A broken selling process maybe. Poor management. Defective products. You name it, they don't want to think about it.

When you don't have extra money lying around, you have to stop and think, *How do I make this work?* People who live within limited means often solve their problems. They usually have no other choice. If things are tight, it's natural to think, *OK, what's the best way to use our funds?* But if you've got excess, where's it being used?

---

[35] "The Science of Quicker Decision Making," Anna Powers, Forbes, April 30, 2018, www.forbes.com/sites/annapowers/2018/04/30/the-science-of-quicker-decision-making/#1cd459e95c9e.

No Follow-Through

When ATS kicked off that semiconductor manufacturer project, their management sent all employees a memo. "We're moving away from our old chemical systems in the cooling towers to a new, chemical-free technology." A classic top-down decision. No one bothered to get employees' buy-in to the initiative. The average worker wasn't committed to helping them (or us) make the switch. We wasted time and energy because no one below senior leadership cared. In fact, most employees treated us like a nuisance. The project would've gone differently had management painted a picture for everybody and secured their buy-in. Think, *What's the reasoning behind this decision? How does this benefit everyone?* rather than *People should obey us because we said so.*

Trends

Utah is known for scenic desert views, good-natured citizens, and multilevel marketing. Whether they sell diet pills or scented candles, MLM companies average a nine-year life cycle. They're hot for the first five years, then decline into ruin. Supply overruns the demand. More people want to sell the product than to buy it. We've all met someone who joined an MLM company toward the end of its run. The last time you visited their house, you may have seen a pile of unopened boxes collecting dust in the corner.

If you're going to chase a hot new trend, you need to start looking on day one for what you're going to do next. What you do today lays down your strategy for the next six to ten years. If you're not spending half your time on what's next after the trend, you don't have a strategy. You're not going to make it after this trend is over.

When I was a teenager, the grapefruit forty-five diet was the big thing. Now it's the ketogenic diet that's trendy. In one of my other companies, we have a customer who sells seven thousand packages of keto supplements a day. Eventually that'll be replaced by something else. If they don't prepare to change now, they won't make the jump. That trend could be a stepping stone to the next one, but more often it becomes a short-lived success story.

Another company I own fulfills product orders. Our clients market the latest products like CBD oil and forward the orders to us for copacking. Then we ship products to their customers. The problem I've found with putting your eggs into one cutting-edge product basket is their often short life span. We can't offer long-term product warehousing and fulfillment contracts because our clients may not be in business tomorrow. Sure, they're moving hundreds of thousands of dollars of product this month, but this may be only a practice run at the latest trend. That business model can't sustain success. The CBD oil craze may last four or five years. Only a few companies will figure out how to be the market leaders. Hundreds of other prospectors will fade.

Products like CBD oil bring quick success to first movers. We learn from failure. We don't learn from success because we often don't know why we're succeeding. More often than not, success gives us an excuse to misuse management and money. When we're coasting on a highly successful new product, we don't think about the future because life's too good. Until it's not. The wave reaches its end, and whoever surfed it too long crash-lands on the shores of reality.

C Players

Nobody ever hires an employee who doesn't fit the company culture or position on purpose. But everyone ends up with some people who don't work out. If you have any kind of leadership role in an organization, it's up to you to hire and keep A players on your team.

You can tell the difference between A players and C players by their enthusiasm. Enthusiasm for what they're doing is different from letting their emotions take over. Enthusiasm is being excited to come to work. They look forward to it. They believe in the product or service. They believe you're going to change the world. They still have to deal with the realities and the ugliness of business, but it's all worth it. Enthusiasm is not just playing the cheerleader and shouting, "Rah-rah." You may employ somebody quiet but passionate about their work. You may get texts from them at ten or eleven at night with real questions. They're not just trying to make you think they work late hours. A players are constantly trying to solve the company's issues for continuous improvements.

Curiosity is another common manifestation of enthusiasm. Somebody who is enthusiastic about their work learns everything they can about it. They want to understand the subject. You can hear the enthusiasm when they talk, even when they don't think they're being heard. A players think about their work all day. At a basketball game, they're thinking about a deal. If they're relaxing in front of the TV, they're pondering a conversation from earlier that day. The gears are turning. Never reject A-player enthusiasm when you see it. C players hide, punch a time clock, and forget about work the second they've punched out. Working with these people comes at a high cost.

A few years ago, ATS got an opportunity to work with the government of Brazil to clean their waterways. A public official referred us to a gentleman, whom I'll call Aaron. Aaron had experience with federal projects around the country. He was also a "super connector" whose relationships could speed up slow-moving bureaucracies. My wife and I flew to Rio de Janeiro, met Aaron, and hired him on the spot to secure meetings with powerful people.

In between meetings with Aaron in Rio, Cara and I met with Padre Omar of the Catholic church at Paróquia Santos Angos in Leblon, a neighborhood in Rio de Janeiro. Padre Omar and his staff needed help revamping the famous Christ the Redeemer statue because of structural damage from an earthquake. Cara and I were considering making a donation to restore this iconic landmark. This was an important project to us because of our belief in and love for Jesus Christ. We were surprised that nowhere around the site or statue were there signs of information about the life and mission of Jesus Christ. The reason for even building this meaningful symbol of God's love is to remind the world of his love. With millions of visitors each year to this site, how could there be no mention of Christ anywhere? At the bottom of the mountain, we saw signs—SPONSORED BY PIRELLI and SPONSORED BY TOYOTA. We thought we'd use some of the proceeds from cleaning the water in the bay for this great project for the Catholic church. We also wanted to help them build a visitor center explaining the life of Christ and why the statue is important. We toured the statue with Padre Omar and viewed some of the damages. Padre Omar also asked us to look at the botanical gardens. They have hundreds of thousands of samples of plants that are only available there. All paper archives. No digital searchability. If we could find a way to digitize that knowledge base, with its many specimens and thousands added every month, we might find a cure for every disease.

A few days after Cara and I paid Padre Omar a visit, Aaron arranged my flight to Brazil's capital city—Brasilia—where I met with senators, ministers, and the president's cabinet. Aaron also connected me to a $43 billion partner back in Rio. This company had the manpower, and my company had the chemistry. I explained to Brazil's leaders that together we would give the twelve million people across Rio safe water for recreation. We received their full support.

As we finalized the funding to start the project, I overheard Aaron on a phone call with an attorney in Brazil, backtracking on things he had told me were done. Aaron tried to bully the attorney, who hadn't been paid to clean up after him. I realized that he hadn't been honest with me. I knew then that I didn't know enough about him. Basic background checks produced nothing, so we completed a criminal background check. Identity theft. Fraud. And worse.

I then caught Aaron setting up a backdoor deal to put millions in his own pocket. I canceled the project. It was disheartening to see the corruption and know we couldn't get involved. I wasted time, energy, and goodwill backing out of the deal. That experience taught me to verify who I work with or, at the very least, who not to work with. C players who have been caught up in criminal activities are the exception. People in general are good, but anytime a person is in the wrong seat or without motivation, even the best shift toward mediocrity. I have learned to never surround myself with C players.

Unfair Consequences

You're living your life. You're trying your best to make good decisions. Then someone else—an employee, client, friend, or family member—blows it. Your operations manager gets angry over nothing and quits without notice. A client believes a rumor planted in the press by a competitor and ends your contract early. Your spouse decides it's time to go your separate ways and insists that the kids won't be staying with you. Whatever the decision and whoever made it, it's now up to you to deal with the consequences. It's not fair, but it happens all the time. I went through a divorce. I've had business relationships that I thought were trustworthy fall apart. Situations with unfair consequences can change the life trajectory you had planned. Most of the time, it's a temporary detour. How temporary? It could be a couple of months—or it could be a decade or more. As long as you respond to the situation with wisdom (and don't make it worse), unfair consequences are obstacles you *can* overcome.

Overstaying

When people stick it out at a job they hate, they beg to get fired. I can't count the number of lies and thefts I've caught unengaged employees saying and making over the years. They should've quit years before I ended up firing them. Did they have to inflate mileage? Double report company expenses? Claim they had new prospects lined up when they didn't? Keep important information to themselves? Sneak behind my back to offer clients a separate contract between the two of them to the tune of millions of dollars? No, but they did anyway. All these ex-employees had to do was come to me and be honest.

"I don't feel like this job is for me. It's time to move on," said one employee, taking the high road.

"OK. I'm happy to help you transition," I said. "I'll call around, help you find an opening, and negotiate your salary and benefits package."

When you stay in a situation longer than you should, you erode trust and suck out opportunities. Don't force yourself to get fired and lose your reputation.

The Third Contaminant—Unproductive Traits

Overoptimism

Early in my career, I bought a couple of partners out of the retail beverage business I'd started. I overpaid the first one. I paid him *twice* what he would have accepted. I know that now because he told me after he took the check! I got a loan to be able to buy the second partner out, which took me two years to pay off. At the time, I just wanted them out of the business because I *knew* I could take it to the next level all by myself. Anyone who didn't share my vision didn't belong.

Within days of signing the paperwork to make me the sole owner of the company, I realized that our entire inventory had expired. The assets were all but worthless. I did sell a few cases of product through secondhand stores, but most of it went to the Utah Food Bank. That way I could help lots of people and take a small tax credit for donating. We can both learn a lesson from my oversight—never get so focused on potential success that you forget the actual risks. As leaders, we feel like we need to have all the answers. Like we need to understand everything. Sometimes we're not willing to take other people's input. This only harms us. We need to be smart enough to realize that we are not smart enough.

Procrastination

Have you ever had a good idea that you never acted on? Everybody gets million-dollar ideas, but we fail to do anything with them. Procrastination is a decision we make to let life happen to us. It's the difference between you paddling your canoe and rafting in the rapids. We've made a decision to procrastinate, and we reinforce it every time we put things off.

When I first met Cara's family, I noticed that several of them took action immediately. If something came to mind, it was accomplished. The first time my father-in-law wanted to introduce me to somebody, he said, "Hey, this is the top guy if you're looking at doing something like a franchise. He's down in the San Diego area. Just a second, I'll get his number for you now." Within a minute and a half, we had the guy on the phone. Most people would say, "Yeah, I'll get back to you. I'll see if I can dig up his name." Not my father-in-law.

If you have a great idea or you want to get something done, make up your mind right now that you're going to do it. Now. Don't wait until it's too late. And yes, there is such a thing as too late. In water treatment, I've seen procrastination cause environmental disasters. Public officials are often so worried that they'll harm either wildlife or the general public that they don't take action. Across North America, mussels and algae are disrupting delicate ecosystems in waterways and lakes. All because we're not taking swift, effective action. Meanwhile, we make rules that don't work, like requiring boaters to rinse off their boats after a ride in the lake. That's cute but ineffective. It's an on-your-honor system, and not every boater is ethical (or sober). If even one boater doesn't clean the bilge or bladder bag or rinse off inflatable toys, they can move invasive species to another lake or waterway. It's happened in Texas.[36] It can happen again anywhere.

Assumptions

"It ain't what we don't know that gets us in trouble. It's the things we know that ain't so." Mark Twain supposedly wrote that, but I'm not going to make any assumptions. To make better decisions, we need to assume that everything we assume is probably wrong.

Too often I see water treatment chemists assume that the rules of chemistry don't apply to their pet product. Once, a new company

[36] "Invasive Zebra Mussel Threat Growing in Canyon Lake," Mitch Hagney, Rivard Report, July 27, 2018, https://therivardreport.com/invasive-zebra-mussel-threat-growing-in-canyon-lake.

promised an innovative and efficient way to run water through cooling towers. They claimed their way did not need chemicals or electricity to function. They ignored chemical laws. Remembering, truth is truth. All matter must obey laws. I knew the system wouldn't work, but reality doesn't stop an entrepreneur with a fantasy. Let me explain.

You probably remember from physical science class that when water evaporates, whatever minerals are in the water stay behind. Such buildings as hospitals or offices evaporate thousands of gallons of water every hour. That evaporation leaves solids behind in the cooling towers—solids that have to be washed away and replaced with fresh water. One chemical company claimed that you could add their magic chemical to tower cooling systems and skip that step. Those who assumed that this company told the truth, believed the claims, purchased the product, and ruined their cooling tower equipment. Solids build up wherever water is evaporated. It turns out chemistry applies even to chemists.

Don't make the same mistake of assuming that rules don't apply to you because you don't want them to.

Overgiving

If you're generous by nature, you need to have some checks and balances to make sure you don't go overboard with compensation. Employees (if you have them) aren't taking the risk you are. They get to go home at night and sleep well. They have not mortgaged their homes, so their houses aren't on the line. Because of your risk, you need to keep an emergency fund so that the next time a vendor goes bankrupt, you can still make payroll.

Remember the military project? The one where the vendor left us twisting in the wind? I learned that the military base wouldn't pay us until the work was completed. I worked with the bank to get financed. I remember sitting in the parking lot trying to eat my sandwich. I felt sick to my stomach over the financial stress this arrangement had caused me. *This is why it's important that I pay people fairly. There are ranges of pay for a given region and position that provide guidance on what is fair. These are similar to the relationship of financial risk and interest rate. The higher the risk, the higher the interest rate. No one should have to go through this stress. If they do, there needs to be a trade-off.*

I continue to improve the checks and balances put in place with my team members so that people are compensated on merit. These checks and balances include discussions with board members, industry data, and salary data banks. I have to remind myself as I deal with the constant stress of payroll and bills, *My employees don't have to deal with this, so it's OK to pay market wages—they're not dealing with the stress I am. At the end of the day, I'll benefit from it.* They didn't have weeks of sleepless nights trying to figure out how to make payroll. I ended up working with about fifteen different banks before we got one that would put the loan together. Still, every small business owner knows that gut-sinking feeling when you wonder if you'll have to cut your salary to zero so that you don't have to lay everyone else off. I was willing to do that so that I could keep my employees' families fed and sheltered, but thankfully it never came to that.

Self-Centeredness

Norway is the sixth-largest producer of hydroelectric power in the world. Farmers across the country are damming up rivers, installing hydroelectric power systems, and selling that energy to fellow Europeans. Central Africans have followed suit, building clean energy dams up and down the Nile River to power cities and villages alike. Civil engineers in the small Himalayan country of Nepal will soon follow.

But what happens when you build a dam, whether you intend to generate hydroelectric power or not? You *dam up* the flow of water. It's the difference between a picture-perfect waterfall and a trickle you can't even see. For centuries, Norway's scenic waterways have attracted wealthy tourists. Many vacationers stroll through local farmers markets and buy fresh produce. As landowners build dams to personally profit from the sale of hydroelectricity, there will be fewer scenic views, less tourism, and a smaller customer base for those who depend on local buyers. It will be interesting to watch the unintended consequences of this trend.

In a similar fashion, in Egypt and across East Asia—Pakistan, India, China—millions of people are going to get angry when they find their fresh water supply cut off by people claiming and altering the current use of the water source. It doesn't take long for hostile citizens to vote war hawks into office. Any time you take care of yourself at the expense of your community or country, everybody loses big.

Now What?

Now that you know about the most common decision contaminants, like fear of success or unfair consequences, you can't ignore their influence. No matter how insignificant they may seem.

I know this decision contaminants list may seem overwhelming. Whenever ATS analyzes wastewater, we find all types of bacteria, pesticides, heavy metals, and worse. Yet it's this crucial knowledge that empowers us to make the right water treatment recommendations. Likewise, over the coming chapters, we'll treat each decision contaminant with a principle or procedure. As a result, you will automatically make better decisions. And you'll no longer have to waste even five minutes identifying and reversing bad decisions. Because you won't be making them anymore.

CHAPTER 4

So We've Made Bad Decisions.

Is It Too Late?

What Makes a Decision Good . . . or Bad

How can you tell clean water from unclean water? Well, you often can't tell by looking at it. If harmful bacteria invisible to the naked eye are in the water, people will get sick. You wouldn't know by looking at it or even by waiting a few minutes after drinking it. But sooner or later, you'll feel the effects. It's the same with decisions. We can't always tell whether a decision was good or bad in the moments or even days after we've made it. That was the case with the first desalination technology.

When you desalinate water, you remove salts and minerals to make it drinkable. All upside, no downside, right? With one technology, you could supply clean water to the world. That's what early desalination proponents expected. Whether desalination benefits everyone depends on what you do with the concentrated salts and minerals removed in the process. Recall that when water evaporates, whatever else that was in the water stays behind. For desalination plants, that whatever else is salts and minerals, called brine. If the plants dump brine back into the ocean too quickly, reefs, plants, fish—everything—suffers or even dies. The public won't notice saltier than usual seas until it's too late. Nobody wants this, but good intentions don't prevent a worst-case scenario. Not in water treatment and not in life. How many times have well-meaning experts told the public something was safe when it wasn't? Remember the sugar-free beverage craze a few years ago? Beverage companies released diet alternatives to sugary sodas. Years after the switch from sugar to saccharin, diet soda drinkers developed symptoms of degenerative diseases.[37] Then we switched to aspartame, which may cause obesity, diabetes, and worse.[38]

We are free and independent agents who can choose how we react. But we don't get to choose our consequences. All we can do is clean

[37] "Could Artificial Sweeteners Be Bad for Your Brain?," Robert H. Shmerling, *Harvard Health Blog*, June 7, 2017, www.health.harvard.edu/blog/could-artificial-sweeteners-be-bad-for-your-brain-2017060711849.
[38] Dagfinn Aune, "Soft Drinks, Aspartame, and the Risk of Cancer and Cardiovascular Disease," *American Journal of Clinical Nutrition* 96, no. 6 (2012): 1249–51.

up our decision-making process today to get better outcomes tomorrow.

But what do I do about all the bad decisions I've made in the past? You're probably thinking. *If I've already made mistakes, is it too late?*

I promise you, it's never too late to reverse a bad decision. To date, I haven't yet studied a water supply so filthy that it can't be made drinkable. If a chemist or engineer made a terrible decision to undertreat or overtreat water, the first thing we do is look for an alternative. That bad decision *can* be undone. So the brilliant minds at ATS go to work to find solutions.

It's the same when you want to reverse a poor decision. Maybe that decision affected only you. Maybe it rippled out across your family, workplace, or community. If you truly desire to correct a bad decision, your brain goes to work on your behalf. Even while you're sleeping, your unconscious mind generates ways to rectify the situation.

Maybe you made a selfish decision at home that hurt a loved one. Maybe it was a decision to compromise your integrity on the job, and you went against your true principles. The consequences will disrupt your life, but you can always get back where you should be. Apologize and remedy the bad behavior. Recommit to your principles. And change whatever policy you made at work that diminished your integrity.

With each escape route you brainstorm, you relieve stress. The pressure fades. You stop feeling paralyzed. You can sleep at night again. Even your thoughts change. *Yes, there* is *a way out of this.* If some of your ideas sound unreasonable, that's all right. What matters is that you are thinking everything through to arrive at a decision. Because it's never too late to start making a change for the better.

The Worst Decision We Can Ever Make

When you realize you've made a bad decision, the worst thing you can do is try to justify it. Do this and you follow the disgraced steps of the Flint, Michigan, officials who mistakenly ruined residents' clean water supply. They had already spent taxpayer money building a new pipeline. If they gave up, it would all be for nothing, they reasoned.

I can understand the reluctance to own up to mistakes you've made. We live in a culture of shame. Public humiliation motivates us to cover up embarrassing choices. We sweep the truth under a sanitized press release or an elaborate explanation. Journalists are often too happy to help. Don't go the way of the modern press, either. In the June 15, 2009, issue of *C&EN Journal,* my father's letter to the editor scolded reporters who bury the truth for the sake of a headline.

> I believe journalism is on a path to its own obsolescence because it is ceasing to be a profession. Journalism no longer seeks the truth. Instead of doing the due diligence to discover truth, there has been a lazy shift toward figuring out what other journalists are thinking and accepting that "consensus" as being truth. This low-effort approach tends to . . . undermine confidence in what used to be a profession. The same thing would happen to science if consensus were accepted as scientific truth.[39]

---

[39] Robert G. Allred, letter to the editor, *C&EN Journal,* June 15, 2009.

Whether journalists or water treatment engineers, we're all responsible for seeking out truth for our own decisions and for what we do after we have made poor ones. When we make poor decisions and stick to them no matter what, we attack our own confidence. We stymie our ability to produce results, and we never experience the immediate peace that comes with a plan to reverse a poor decision and repair harmed relationships. The quicker we acknowledge our mistakes and make corrections, the sooner we get our confidence back so that we can make things right. As acclaimed management expert Jim Collins said, let's "deal with the brutal facts."[40] We can reverse a bad decision when we're real with ourselves and look at the facts—but not when we try to reinterpret a bungle as brilliance.

It's natural to feel like hiding from your mistakes, but you can only flee the consequences for so long. So why run? The restored gospel of Jesus Christ is a message of repentance, which means to change your behavior forever. When we recognize that we did something wrong, we can learn from it by making a change to align our behavior with the will of God. We then try with all our might to never make that mistake again. Isn't that why we're on this earth? To learn? I believe that life is a university. We "go to school" every day. Yes, it takes time to reflect on what you could improve, without beating yourself up. My belief is that God wants us to become better each day so that we can get the most out of life. That doesn't mean the most money or the most fun; it means that we learn all we can and build healthy relationships. Learning is

---

[40] "Confront the Brutal Facts," Jim Collins, accessed September 30, 2019, www.jimcollins.com/concepts/confront-the-brutal-facts.html.

success. Even if it's a painful lesson that requires repentance for us to move forward.

I imagine that if you sat in the Sears boardroom twenty years ago, you would have heard ideas that could have reversed their retail market share decline. Perhaps even ideas good enough to beat Walmart. Most people in that room probably didn't want to rock the boat. Why risk shareholder scorn with a radical plan to turn around the business that might fail? So Sears chose the only path that all but guaranteed the company's demise. Sears kept prices so high that they lost customers to Walmart; meanwhile, profits plummeted, and company stock lost 96 percent of its value.[41] It wasn't too late to avoid bankruptcy . . . until it was.

I'm not saying those Sears guys' fears about trying a radical new plan were unfounded. When you make the decision to reverse a previous one, you'll often find your new decision unpopular. When a company president, government official, or religious leader charts a new course, the masses don't always buy in. People who aren't close to the situation can't see down the road. That is exactly what makes good leaders stand out. They have a thirty-thousand-foot view of the direction in which things need to go and are brave enough to lead. Even if the decision goes against the flow of popular opinion. So how far into the future are you looking? Can you help others see what you see? Are you willing to right the wrongs of the past, no matter how painful and unpopular it might be?

---

[41] "Who Killed Off Sears? Fifty Years on the Road to Ruin," Shoshanna Delventhal, Investopedia.com, July 1, 2019, www.investopedia.com/news/downfall-of-sears.

It doesn't matter what people think, what the popular opinion is, or what some self-proclaimed expert wrote on social media. Good decisions are always principle based. You do the right thing *because* it's the right thing. If you don't take right and wrong into consideration, your decision will be short lived or cause more harm than good down the road. If those water treatment professionals went along with what was popular and ignored natural and chemical laws, think what the consequences would be.

Several years ago, ATS invested nearly $1 million in a new technology out of Israel that (I believed) would save the average hospital thirty-six million gallons of water a year. Industry publications, politicians, and news desks gave glowing reviews of the technology. I couldn't pass up the opportunity to bring this green technology into water treatment. After five years of running this expensive equipment, we started to see some unexplained issues. We ran tests to confirm that everything worked as promised. It did—but not consistently. We talked it over as a leadership team, and we decided that we could not in good conscience let our customers use it. So we pulled the plug on the new tech. We spent the next five years paying back the loan with nothing to show for it. Nobody said course correction was easy. But it's easy to imagine the alternative. If hospitals used our unpredictable system to cool such critical spaces as operating rooms, we could've seen catastrophe. Imagine a physician performing a lifesaving surgery when all of a sudden the room heats up everything and everyone—surgical equipment, attending nurses, the patient on the table. I would rather be stuck paying off debt than compromise the safety of even just one operation.

That lesson did pay off. A few years later, I structured another deal for ATS. I shared with Cara how the terms would benefit everyone involved.

"Isn't it nice that you had all those other experiences to learn from?" she said. "Those lessons got you to this point. You're in a wiser, more cautious position than before. Now you're negotiating a contract that will benefit you, the company, our family, and the families of everyone who works with ATS and the client."

Cara was right. This new opportunity came from getting it wrong before. Instead of continuing to get it wrong, we thought about our mistakes and evaluated each new decision. *What would I do differently next time? How could I become better at this?*

Not every lesson is profitable. Sometimes doing the right thing costs more than we could imagine. On April 5, 1993, in Milwaukee, Wisconsin, something strange happened. Grocery stores, pharmacies, and doctors' offices ran out of antidiarrheal and antinausea medicine. Thousands of calls to the Milwaukee Health Department led water treatment engineers to the culprit. Cryptosporidium protozoan.[42] This single-celled parasite somehow survived the city's water filtration process. Two days later, Milwaukee Water Works ordered a boil advisory. But not before more than four hundred thousand residents got sick from cryptosporidiosis—diarrhea, nausea, stomach cramps, fever. More than eighty people died.

---

[42] "Cryptosporidium and Public Health," Kathleen Blair, *Drinking Water and Health Newsletter,* March 1, 1995, waterandhealth.org/newsletter/old/03-01-1995.html.

Engineers got to work reviewing the city's water treatment process and recommended upgrades. Whatever allowed these parasites to remain in the water had to be stopped no matter the cost. It wasn't cheap. Upgraded treatment plants and enhanced disinfection systems ran up an $89 million bill. (Let's take a moment to be grateful that everyday bad decisions don't risk human life or cost a fortune.)

Even if your decisions don't affect millions, they can and do impact people you care about for the rest of their lives. If you're in a position of leadership, you can help those around you learn from their mistakes and turn failures into steps toward success. Throughout my career, I've chosen to fire underperforming employees with dignity. I help them understand a few reasons why I've decided to part ways in a kind manner. I always meet with the person eye to eye unless urgency and distance make it impossible. ATS offers a reasonable severance to help them land on their feet, yet not so reasonable that they feel like they don't have to work again. If possible, I also provide a reference letter. I've even asked friends to help former employees find someplace else to work.

Some people understand that water treatment isn't a good fit for them and appreciate my help. Not everyone. I've noticed that the more prideful an employee is, the less likely they are to want help. They get irritated when I tell them that we need to talk in private. I can see their thoughts on their faces—*Nobody has the right to fire me!* (Often they tell me so with gusto.) Yet most employees I've let go come back months or years later. They tell me about what they're doing and how life got better after the sting of being fired faded. The opportunity to change their attitude or behavior in a new environment brought them the success they wanted.

Honesty almost always leads to positive change. We can learn a lot about how to make good decisions from what caused us to make bad ones. Still, justifying, blaming, and becoming the victim feels easier than dealing with the causes of bad decisions. But it's not productive in the long run. Every contaminated water supply has its own unique mix of chemicals, heavy metals, and organic compounds that we need to treat. Each of us has our own blend of emotions, situations, and traits that drive bad decisions. What negative emotions got you stirred up before you yelled at your spouse? What compromising situations did you get stuck in when you spent money you didn't have? What unproductive traits have become a habit you can't break when a big project is on the line?

If we want clean water, we have to study each contaminant and recommend a specific treatment. If water treatment engineers said, "You know, this chemical will *probably* kill any *E. coli* bacteria that got into the water. Let's use it," we would ruin civilization. At one time, water treatment engineers didn't know that arsenic or lead were a problem. They let chemicals and heavy metals travel through the system all the way to the tap. Luckily, over time, technology in developed nations advanced. We went from measuring toxic compounds in parts per million to parts per billion to parts per trillion in some cases. We can tell when even the tiniest amount of poison shows up in the water supply.

Nature herself offers a better example than anything we humans have ever developed. Do our planet's rolling waters remain impure? The water cycle is amazing to watch. In Brazil, Cara and I have been able to see much of the cycle in person. The evaporation of ocean water. The majestic evaporation of the tropical Atlantic Forest high above Rio de Janeiro. To the sheer show of force at Iguazu Falls, with her hundreds of breathtaking waterfalls canvasing cliffs as they press ever toward that ocean where the water cycle begins again. In life, we can correct behavior, repent (change), and move forward. Just as water's movement prevents stagnation. As we move forward with our best efforts, we keep ourselves from becoming victims of our own choices.

Reversing bad decisions is possible, but going forward, why risk it? Rectifying these situations takes a lot of your time—40 percent of it, actually. This is time you'd probably rather spend enjoying your life. If we want to fix our bad decisions and start making good ones, we have to recognize that we made a mistake, learn from it, and change our behavior. Then we need to assign a specific process to keep those decision contaminants out of our lives going forward. In the chapters ahead, I won't only give you the tools to make good decisions your norm, but I'll help you prevent wasted time in the future.

CHAPTER 5

The Case for the Fundamentals

How Ultrapure Water Saved Lives and Created the Internet

D o you remember where you were when you heard that the trapped Chilean miners were rescued? I do. On October 13, 2010, I was at a water purification systems trade show in Salt Lake City. After a world record sixty-four days trapped underground, the first rescued miner appeared in front of the cameras. I was one of a billion people watching. Family members, Chilean officials, and fellow miners embraced all thirty-three rescued souls. It was as if they'd come back from the dead. You may not have watched the rescue happen live, but you probably followed the headlines.

Behind every miracle are good people making smart decisions at the right time as well as a loving father in heaven. What happened after the fateful cave-in at Chile's San José copper and gold mine was no different.[43] Blocked by tons of fallen rock three miles down in the mine, the miners had no way out. Another group closer to the entrance escaped up the spiraling underground ramps. The other thirty-three didn't.

The escaped miners sent word back to company leadership, who notified the government. Over the next forty-eight hours, a rescue team mobilized. Even NASA and American corporations like Northrop Grumman (an ATS client) got involved. On Thursday, August 5, a second cave-in trapped the miners in a cloud of dust for six hours. Fallen rock kept rescuers blocked from the main entryway, the most obvious route of escape. Removing the debris risked a third (and deadly) cave-in. There was a lot of it. Unlike open pit mines in the western United States, many of Chile's mines are underground—and big. So big that full-size mining trucks drive in and out. So with the main rescue route blocked, people had to get creative. The rescue team decided on a heavy machinery solution. They would drill grapefruit-size boreholes down into the earth.

---

[43] "Eight Hours of Rescue Brings Eight Miners Freedom," CNN, October 13, 2010, http://news.blogs.cnn.com/2010/10/13/workers-begin-to-rescue-trapped-chilean-miners/?hpt=T1&iref=BN1.

Why so small? If they bored holes any bigger without knowing where the miners were, they might have caused another collapse.

It took about two weeks to drill from the surface down to the depth where the miners were—twenty-three hundred feet below ground. That's equal to 233 stories. Finally, on August 22, drill operators felt tapping on their perforation. When they withdrew the drill bit, they found a note attached: "*Estamos bien en el refugio, los 33*" ("We are well in the shelter, the 33 of us"). Chile celebrated, and the world with them.

Rescuers sent water, medicine, and nutrient-dense food down the tiny shaft to sustain the men. Meanwhile, the drilling team bored a much larger hole down to the trapped miners. This one fit an adult-size rescue capsule. It sounds easier than it was. The drilling team had to drill down, jot out around solid rock, and then drill back toward the miners. A Northrop Grumman gyroscope—a digital drill bit ax guidance system—was the only technology that offered precise control. The gyroscope kept the machine operators from triggering another cave-in as they cleared tons and tons of rock. Once they drilled through to the miners, rescuers dropped the capsule down and winched the miners to the surface one by one.

Everyone involved in the rescue deserves credit. From the drill operators who removed solid rock with care, to the miners who kept their spirits up for sixty-four days. But the story of one little hero that made the once-in-a-lifetime rescue possible has never been told until now. That hero is ultrapure water.

ATS has had a contract with Northrop Grumman for over thirty-five years to produce ultrapure water. How pure is ultrapure? We can measure its purity down to 0.056 microsiemens/cm2. The water is so pure that it would leech copper out of copper pipes. Ultrapure water is also used to manufacture microchips for your cell phone and your computer.

It was that ultrapure water that helped make the electronic components that guided the drill, which ultimately dug out the miners. Without the gyroscope, drilling teams wouldn't have been able to rescue the miners or prevent a third cave-in.

What's the connection between ultrapure water and a drilling guidance system? Imagine throwing a handful of sand on your kitchen table before you eat. You've got to clean that sand off before you set the table. When you make computer chips (such as those for a gyroscope), you etch the board. That leaves impurities on the surface of the board. It's even worse than trying to clean that sand off your table. Even the teeniest particle of dust could block electricity. The chips are washed in five to seven ultrapure baths to get them clean down to parts per trillion. Any particles left over from the etching collect in that ultrapure water. Every gallon we make and use for these baths is discarded because of the impurities. And if that wasn't enough to wrap your head around, every chip goes through five etching processes, requiring five to seven ultrapure water baths each time.

I'll understand if you nodded off during that paragraph. Ultrapure water baths aren't glamorous, but without them, we wouldn't have the World Wide Web, GPS, smartphones, or other essentials of our daily lives. We'd be stuck using tech from the 1960s. As for the Chilean miners, their story might have ended inside that mine. ATS wasn't directly involved with the miner rescue, but we provided the ultrapure water that made the gyroscope possible. Look behind any spectacular rescue story. What do you see? When people execute the fundamentals of their profession—and of good decision-making—life improves. Fundamentals are never spectacular until they're essential.

Making Clutch Decisions without Thinking Twice

When you first played sports as a kid, you learned about fundamentals. If you played basketball, you practiced dribbling with your right hand, with your left hand, and then back and forth. You practiced keeping the ball away from defenders. You practiced shooting from the free-throw line. All fundamentals of basketball. Do all those right when you're on the court by yourself, and nobody thinks anything of it. But when Michael Jordan dribbles down the court against the Utah Jazz, keeps the ball away from Jazz defender Byron Russell, and makes a jump shot from the free-throw line to win his sixth championship, fans remember it for the rest of their lives. The fundamentals are boring . . . until they're not.

I played basketball quite a bit when I was younger. Even as a sophomore in high school, we did the same drills we learned as eight-year-olds. That's how important the basics were. During games, I executed those fundamentals without thinking about them. When I shot a basket, I didn't think about proper shooting, such as "Keep your arm bent, elbow in, eye on the target, and follow through." The fundamentals were automatic because I spent so much time practicing them.

The same goes for every sport. Anyone can hit a few good golf shots on the range when nobody is watching and you're not counting your strokes. It's the same with the decisions you and I make every day. Can you stay calm when your computer crashes five minutes before a big presentation? Let anger take over, and you may lose the deal you've worked for your entire career. But if you practice the fundamentals of anger management, they become automatic. It's second nature to keep a clear head, figure out a plan B, and ace the presentation. These little moments of truth add up over a lifetime. It may not feel like it when you're in them, but they shape your destiny. Do you become the professional, the partner, and the person you've always aspired to be? Or do your emotions get the better of you?

An entrepreneur once asked me, "How do you stay so in control? You're always calm. Me? I'm always panicking. My business is growing so fast, it's putting cash constraints on what I can do."

"Focus on the fundamentals. Think of it like your morning routine," I said. "There are certain things you do no matter what. No matter how stressed you are, you take a shower, brush your teeth, comb your hair, say your prayers, and read your scriptures. If you take care of the fundamentals of emotion management, good decisions take care of themselves. That way when we get into an unfamiliar scenario, we go back to the basics without even thinking about it."

"That makes a lot of sense." He nodded. "But what are the fundamentals of managing my emotions? What should I be doing every day to prepare myself for stressful situations?"

Great question. In the chapters ahead, I'll share the fundamentals of good decision-making that mentors, clients, and luck (both good and bad) have taught me. Each method, process, and tip will help you make more productive, more rewarding decisions automatically. How? These fundamentals neutralize the emotions, situations, and traits that could contaminate a decision. I pair each solution with a contaminant it treats best. As these fundamentals become second nature, you'll find that what works on one contaminant works on others as well. In the water treatment process, chlorine kills such bacteria as salmonella and *E. coli* as well as many deadly viruses.

As with drills, if we practice decision-making fundamentals when the stakes are low, we make "clutch" decisions under pressure. The time to try out these methods, processes, and tips is not five minutes before the big meeting or when your spouse says, "We need to talk." It's now. In the routine of life.

Most of us never have an experience like Saul on the road to Damascus. A bright light, a visitation from heaven, an instant transformation. Instead, our lives, relationships, and careers improve choice by choice and action by action. Small decisions based on the fundamentals make a person (or a company) great. Years ago, the 3G group out of Brazil flew to Bentonville, Arkansas, to meet billionaire Walmart founder Sam Walton. Sam picked up the 3G executives—

Jorge Paulo Lemann, Marcel Herrmann Telles, and Carlos Alberto Sicupira—in his old pickup truck. After loading his guests' luggage into his truck, Sam kicked off the conversation.

"Let me guess. You three are here to figure out how Walmart became an overnight success." Sam laughed. "Let's start at the beginning— twenty-five years ago."

And such is life. Nobody achieves success and then starts acting the part. The work comes first. Often a long time before you need it to pay off. But if you don't make the right decision when it's easy, you won't when it's difficult. Practice the fundamentals of good decisions every day until you master them. Someday soon you'll be in that high-stakes situation, and your split-second decision will be the correct one. And who knows? Maybe a billion people will be watching.

CHAPTER 6

The Fundamentals of Emotion-Free Decision-Making

How Bad Decisions Wash Over Us

Did you ever play in a stream as a kid? Maybe you chased frogs, fished, or tried to skip rocks. Remember when you stepped into the cold, clear water? Seconds before, you saw everything on the bottom. Algae, pebbles, maybe a shy crayfish. Then a cloud engulfed you, and you couldn't even see your feet.

A similar thing happens when emotions take over a decision. One moment you're thinking clearly, then all of a sudden fear stirs up your thoughts. It's almost impossible to decide what to do. Whatever emotion comes over you, it has you grabbing at whatever choice *feels* right. Maybe you feel anger, so you lash out. You feel greed, so you take without asking. Or you feel proud, so you put others in their place. All the while you don't realize that you're sinking deep into unintended consequences. Only when the negative emotion settles minutes or even days later do you see the damage done.

The good news is that we don't have to let emotions walk all over us, kicking up clouds of confusion when we need a clear head. Preventing negative emotions from soiling decisions starts with awareness of those emotions. Say you're about to make a decision. What emotion comes over you? What sudden urge do you feel that you can't explain? What does that feeling make you want to say or do?

If you don't notice what state of mind you're in when you make a decision, you have little chance of making the right one. Being self-aware and honest is crucial in the process. That goes for everything from choosing a beverage for your meal to choosing who you'll marry. Often I ask myself, *Which emotion is influencing what I'm thinking about right now?* Greed feels a heck of a lot different from anger or fear, for example. As long as you're aware of an emotion, you're able to self-regulate. You can defer to the fundamentals that you know *work*. In this chapter, I'm going to teach you those fundamentals. Practice these today, and keep practicing them. The next time a negative emotion wades into your head, you'll do the right thing. That goes for choosing club soda instead of the sugary caffeinated beverage and for marrying the person who helps you to be the best version of yourself.

Treating Fear

The leap of faith to overcome fear of the unknown does get easier the more you do it. I remember when I hired my first assistant at ATS just before I bought the company from my father. I realized that it was going to cost $2,000 a month to hire her part time. If I didn't increase our revenue to make up for the new payroll expense, I couldn't justify keeping her. I was afraid, but I took the leap anyway. What helped was not committing too much too soon. Once it was clear that my assistant freed me up to be more productive, I committed to more growth. I hired more people. Fast-forward to today, and I have no problem hiring new employees with healthy salaries during the slow months. I know that it takes an employee a few months to be productive. If they're going to be productive when I need them most, I have to take a leap of faith *now*. I used to be scared of $2,000. Now I can add several grand to payroll without losing much sleep. Try treating your fear by taking action. Even little steps bring you forward.

As you take each small step, I encourage you to not take counsel from your fears. Over the last couple of years, ATS has moved toward serving more global customers with bigger budgets. That means we've had to shut down some of our older, smaller contracts to make time for them. Turning down a sure thing (like an existing contract) would be hard for any leader to do, but it's an important thing to learn to do. Even though we may feel afraid, we know that we can better serve our employees, our clients, and the world's need for clean water by shifting the way we do business. I can't see what will happen five years down the road, but I can take a leap of faith and bet the company's time and resources on what I think is best for the future of everyone involved.

Of course, it's hard to take a leap of faith when you're plagued with uncertainty. Leaders show their value when they make the right decision, even if the correct one isn't obvious. To find courage, think about what and who in your life makes you feel safe. Try to connect to that person or place to replenish your reserves and strengthen your ability to fight your fears. Maybe it's coming home to your spouse or going to your mom's house for dinner. My father-in-law had an uncle who used to tell him, "If you ever hit a hard time, there's always a place for you in my home. There will be a warm bed and food on the table if you need it." He never stayed with his uncle, but *knowing* he had a place he could go gave him courage to make bold choices in his career.

Do you have a safe place in your life? If no one offered you such a spot, try offering one to someone else. When you do for others what you would want them to do for you, you make the world better for everyone—including you. By focusing on others' needs, you're able to keep your own problems and challenges in perspective. When we give, we receive in return more than what we gave. We're blessed many times over.

Once you make your decision and act in spite of your fear, you'll be surprised by how much difficulty you can handle without breaking a sweat. One of my colleagues currently has twenty-six lawsuits against him. Most people in that situation would never get a good night's rest again. But for this man, getting sued is simply part of doing business. Another businessman I know used others' fear of litigation to his advantage. For years, his company struggled to win government contracts. Instead of giving up, he decided to be the best qualified bidder and then sue the government and the company wrongfully awarded the contract so that he could legally claim a slice of the pie. Everybody involved backed off. They feared his eight in-house attorneys, who understood contract law and the RFQ (request for quotation) requirements better than anyone involved. I know this seems sinister, and I am not endorsing this strategy. The point is that when you conquer fear that debilitates others, you have the advantage in just about any situation.

Never let fear tell you what you can't do. It's probably hard to succeed, but is it *too* hard? Things could go wrong, but *will* they? Fear says *yes* and *always*. In my experience, reality says *no, not usually*. The next time you find yourself faced with fear, acknowledge it, get in a safe state of mind, and only then make your decision—and take that leap of faith. Decide that you will figure it out and overcome.

Treating Greed

Working with the nonprofit Empower Mali has shown me how greed can take hold on a global scale and devastate less fortunate countries. Empower Mali builds schools, educates local children, and provides school supplies, among other charitable activities. Where possible, Empower Mali also offers solar electricity and water treatment to remote villages with no power grid or clean water infrastructure. We believe everyone on this planet deserves a basic education and clean drinking water.

My work with Empower Mali made me vividly aware of the need for help with clean water in the country of Mali, Africa. In 2019, in conjunction with Utah Mountain Stars, a group of basketball players and parents from Utah sponsored and engaged in a clean water project in a small village outside of Bamako, Mali, called Moussalabougou. Kirk Langston represented ATS. Under his direction, a group of people performed the project installation of the drinking water system. They deployed a simple water filtration and sanitization device designed by the wonderful people on our team back in Utah. This technology delivered clean drinking water to the village for the first time in its history. The village was equipped with a working water well, a water storage tank, and a distribution point. Because no electrical grid was available, solar panels were installed to run continuously, as was a solar-powered pump to treat the raw well water and two sensors—one to shut the pump off if the water table drops below the pump level and one to shut the pump off if the water is about to overflow the tank.

As water flows from the well, it runs through a three-stage filtration process to remove all particles. The water then flows through a solar-powered ultraviolet lamp chamber where the UV light sterilizes any bacteria. Following the UV system, the water flows to the storage tank. The team on the ground was able to use chlorine bleach to disinfect the storage tank and distribution lines. They flushed the system to wash out the residual chlorine so that the new system would be ready for operation. The system was left a full year of replacement filters, and the villagers have been trained on how to maintain the system going forward.

"I cannot describe how much gratitude the little village of Moussalabougou poured out for what we did for them. It's unfortunate that not everyone shares our motive to help the continent," Kirk reported on his return. It changed him and it changed the rest of the team whose hard work makes this type of project possible.

Greed leads us to believe that every deal is a zero-sum game. Somebody wins, somebody loses. I've even met people here in the United States who tell me, "If I make a donation to your charity, I'm just making somebody else wealthy." Greed lies. Sharing has the opposite effect. If you enrich a city or country, everybody benefits. When we educate villagers in remote parts of Mali, we're not just doing something charitable; we're bettering ourselves. It's a win-win deal. In the next fifty years or so, we'll see the people of Mali affording our products and services. Sub-Saharan Africa is already the world's fastest-growing mobile device market. Their purchasing power is a direct result of investments to educate them, improve their health, and lift them from poverty. It takes time, but it's worth it for everyone in the end.

This isn't mere opinion. In *Factfullness: Ten Reasons We Are Wrong about the World—and Why Things Are Better Than You Think*, social scientist Hans Rosling tells us that escape from poverty benefits everyone.[44] Have you ever heard of the four categories of poverty? Whenever a population rises from one category to the next, the whole of humanity is a little bit better off.

- Category 1 poverty: You walk miles for water every day. Staying alive consumes daily life. If you don't work one day, you'll die the next.

- Category 2 poverty: You suffer from life-threatening diseases because you can afford sugary, processed foods but not medical care. If you fall ill and miss a day of work, you and your family could drop down to category one.

- Category 3 poverty: You can take a vacation. You don't have every modern convenience, but you don't have to worry about clean water or unaffordable health care.

- Category 4 poverty: You're in the educated middle class.

Most of Sweden was stuck in category one at the turn of the twentieth century. Today, Swedes are in the fourth category. There was no win-lose. Their progress didn't make any neighboring country worse off. In fact, their economic success amplified what they can buy from trading partners in Scandinavia. The same is possible in areas struggling with water. If we

---

[44] Hans Rosling, *Factfulness: Ten Reasons We're Wrong about the World—and Why Things Are Better Than You Think* (New York: Flatiron Books, 2018).

can help the eighteen million people of Mali meet their basic needs, we can move them to a higher category. Sharing the wealth makes everybody better off. When more people are educated, we all experience less strife. When everyone thrives, everyone wins.

I believe that if a deal doesn't work for both parties, it's not a good deal. If you're outsmarting or taking advantage of somebody, you'll be stuck in a hostile relationship. Nobody wants to work that way. Good CEOs understand that the gate needs to swing both ways. When you're open in your discussions, you learn how you can succeed and make a healthy profit. Taking this approach will put both of you on the same team.

Money is also not a zero-sum game. It's OK for everybody in my supply chain to make a profit. I have learned that our company needs to be fair, and the free market keeps us fair. We can't gouge people. In some cases, ATS works with generational companies. We're selling to the children of clients or customers we sold to years ago. Our deals are relationship based, and our clients need to know that they're going to make money, too. We have a certain margin we need to make to distribute and sell a product, and we're not ashamed to do that. Nobody has to lose money or operate at minimum profits for another party to succeed. That's why we invite vendors to join our sales calls. I don't have any secrets— they know what I sell their product at. They also know I put money into selling our (or their) products. I'm growing their business as well as mine. Deals in which suppliers are pressured to provide their products or services at near cost make customer service and innovation suffer. Ask any original Rubbermaid employee about their love affair with Walmart and the race to the bottom. Rubbermaid played Walmart's game of lowerer than healthy margins to the point that their meeting Walmart's demands forced their sale.[45] Bad business practices opens the door to competition in the same way that a race to the lowest margin destroys futures.

Cooperation and transparency are our advantage. They keep greed from souring a deal. Sometimes people are surprised when I'm so open with what we want and what we feel is fair. But I don't skirt around the issue or try to position ATS to win at any cost. The more transparent we are with our vendors, the more rapport we build. If we hold a discussion with somebody else who may be a vendor's competitor, we shoot straight with each other. I've done some deals overseas that our suppliers here wouldn't have otherwise known about, but I don't want to hide anything. I want them to understand what I'm doing. I don't ask for permission, but I make them aware so that there's never a "gotcha" moment. I have found that greed can't live long when it's brought to light.

In *Blueprint to a Billion*, David G. Thomson reveals how small companies reach a billion dollars in revenue by partnering with a large corporation capable of scaling demand.[46] The smaller business brings the innovation the corporation lacks and needs to stay ahead of the competition. In return, they leverage the corporation's resources. We've

---

[45] "Newell Buying Rubbermaid in $5.8 Billion Deal," Claudia H. Deutsch, *New York Times,* October 22, 1998, www.nytimes.com/1998/10/22/business/newell-buying-rubbermaid-in-5.8-billion-deal.html.

[46] David G. Thomson, *Blueprint to a Billion: 7 Essential to Achieve Exponential Growth* (Hoboken, NJ: Wiley).

used a similar strategy to grow ATS. We partner with vendors that manufacture high-quality products but underperform on selling them. We team up and give them the sales they lack, and they supply excellent products for our customers. We expand their business and by default ours as well. We've grown one vendor's water treatment chemistry sales by 42 percent just this past year. They have fifteen other distributors on the East Coast that grew their businesses by only a combined 20 percent. Probably because they're embarrassed to charge for the value they're providing. Yet they make half the profit margin that ATS does. In another vendor partnership, I sent one of our technical guys to their company to help them manufacture at a faster rate. They increased their product output. We went from roughly a twenty-two week delivery to a four-week delivery. It cost us money to pay our employee's salary, but at the end of the day, we win and so does our vendor. We've also inserted a salesperson and our sales method into a supplier's company. We've set up a sales recording system and assist in their sales efforts. I live by this motto in my business and my family: "A victory for one has to be a victory for all."

We've also found ways to mitigate greed *inside* the company. It starts with having honorable managers. In the past, I've had managers who took a percent of sales and gave out an equal monthly bonus to everyone in the office. Then I had one situation where an executive divided the bonus according to salary. Because he made $200,000 a year and the assistants made $15 an hour, he kept most of the money. This went against the philosophy I try to cultivate in the company and I had to fire him. Good leaders don't operate that way; they always put their team first.

I believe in rewarding a good day's work so that jealousy never festers into greed. Another form of greed is taking credit when credit isn't due. "I want the credit for this," or " I should be rewarded. It was my idea." It's not about money, but it's still greed because you're stealing recognition that belongs to someone else. In my desk at work, I keep a drawer full of gift cards to restaurants and places that a lot of people wouldn't normally fit into their budgets to go to. When an employee does something good, I want to reward them on the spot. I pass them out openly without seeking public acknowledgment. It reinforces people's behavior and builds their self-esteem. People with high self-esteem perform better. Most people can do more than they're ever asked if they have the opportunity to do so.

Treating Pride

I grew up hearing that Pelé was the greatest soccer player of all time. In the documentary *In Search of Greatness,* the interviewer asked Pelé who the greatest soccer player of all time was. Of course, I thought he would say, "Me." Instead he listed off three other soccer players he respected and considered better. Then he added, "I learned from my dad that you're not better than anybody. Don't ever forget that. That's the most important thing you'll ever learn in soccer."

Like Pelé, true leaders in business and in life know they're not better than anyone. While serving a mission for the Church of Jesus Christ of

Latter-day Saints in Brazil, I heard Pelé talked about in every city I visited. When I got back home to Utah, a friend asked me, "So are the people in Brazil good or bad?"

"São Paulo has a lot of people," I said. "Anytime you have twenty million people living together, you're going to have one or two bad ones. I believe that most people are good people. The vast majority of people want the same thing. They want a roof over their heads, food in their bellies, and good health. They want love. They want a good life for their families and good things for their kids. And they hope they get grandkids someday."

Pride makes us forget that we're no better than the next guy, even if we are financially or geographically better off. Pride also fails to remind us of our limits. If you entertain the feeling that you're better than your colleagues or competitors, you assume that you're more capable than you probably really are.

Humble leaders understand their bandwidth and don't stretch themselves too far beyond it. I once hired a sales executive to run our water treatment and safety divisions. After a month of work, he said to me, "These two units are too much for me right now. Can we hire somebody to give me some help on one of them? I'll focus on one until I understand it."

This executive cared more about doing a good job than about building his own kingdom inside the company. Giving up half his domain meant foregoing half his override commissions, the small percentage commission a sales manager receives for his team's performance. But he knew it was in the best interests of the company and our customers. If he'd allowed pride to cloud his perspective, I expect he would not be working for me today. He now runs both the water treatment and safety divisions. His humility allows him to learn, and everyone benefits from it.

Good leaders don't let their pride ruin them or anyone alongside them. If you have employees, students, or children, let them risk failure. If you never let people fail, they'll never be allowed to raise their confidence and abilities. We learn as we fail. My father taught me that helping somebody progress means putting them in a situation above their capability. Then you let them figure it out. There may be setbacks or even failures, but if they have the right attitude, they'll learn to adjust. Their mistakes may reflect poorly on you, which is why many authorities don't let their direct reports make any important decisions. *I know best, not you. I need to look good here.* That's pride talking.

In May 2012, my father and I were still colleagues. As the founder, CEO, and lead chemist, he was the sharpest boss you could ever hope to work alongside. He could do ten to twenty times more water titration tests in a period of time than any other chemist I encountered. All while keeping track of the test results and readings and learning as he went. My dad is truly amazing! He'd look through chemical formulas and pick out errors, reading fourteen to seventeen hundred words a minute. (In technical material, the average reading rate is fifty to seventy-five words a minute.) One longtime employee said my dad had a third-degree black belt in chemistry. If so, he was the calmest sensei anyone ever met. He could work through complex problems better than anyone at the company. Yet with his patience and ability to think forward, he always stepped back and let employees do the job. Even when, at times, it took ten times longer. He knew that one day he would no longer run the company. Everyone around him would need to know how to handle both petty challenges and industry-threatening crises. Sometimes my father's management style lost opportunities. Other times, he lost money. But he never put a subordinate in the position of ruining the company. I always knew he had the ability to pull back the reins when needed.

Take this lesson from my father. As with all things, risk failure in moderation. Don't test your team or your kids when failure means they'll bankrupt your company or burn your house down. Something must be done with exactness. However, in a business and at home, there are things to get done that don't matter *how* they get done, just that they do. These are the perfect opportunities to let people learn and be creative. Some people may work best from 11:00 p.m. to 3:00 a.m. As long as they understand the goal, I'm willing to let them get creative, figure it out, and learn. Some mistakes will get made, sure. They may come back and ask for guidance, and that's OK. When an employee messes up and learns, keep them around. Be willing to correct, coach, and instruct before and after the fact. Not in a punitive manner but by asking, "How could we have done this differently? What things should we consider in the future? and What was learned from this experience?" Failure is your lab, your crucible, your incubator. Policies and procedures for quality control are great, but you still need to let people think and make decisions. Even part-time employees, interns, and assistants. Otherwise, they'll always be a fifteen-dollar-an-hour worker.

Our CFO says that when someone leaves ATS, they should leave with a payout, personal growth, or, whenever possible, both. Part of running a company or managing people is to train and develop leaders. For me, swallowing pride and letting employees (and my children) learn as they fail is a spiritual act. I believe that each of us is given agency by God, meaning that we get to choose our path. It's not forced on us. Even if our parents divorced or abused us or we came from poverty, we still get to decide how we act as a spouse and a parent ourselves.

As leaders, when we let people fail, we're allowing them to use their God-given agency. One of the most inspiring and amazing documents, the US Constitution, does not bestow rights. It simply acknowledges those divine rights granted and the limit of which the US nation is willing to exercise at this time. When we let employees, students, or children exercise their rights, they spread their wings and see how far they can go. God does that with us. He's given us scriptures, the prophets, and of course our agency. There is no mandate within the Church of Jesus Christ that members must do this or must do that. We're taught what to do and what God wants from us, but we can still use our agency. The same is true in a professional setting. Employees and colleagues have their agency as well. What they choose affects us.

A good way to control pride is to remind yourself that you're not better than anyone else. Know when to be humble and ask for help.

Seek ways to serve others. When you model and reinforce these behaviors, you will see others follow in your footsteps.

Treating Shame

Let's say you let emotions get the better of you. You act on fear, anger, or pride, and you do something stupid. When you see the consequences of your actions, you feel ashamed. Acknowledge that you made a poor choice. You could have handled things differently or said something better. Admit that you were wrong, then get the help you need to make it right. If you try to cover up your mistake, you'll make even more. Trust me: one mess is much easier to clean up than three, four, or more.

When we seek to hide or cover up our error, it starts a pattern that sends us in a downward spiral. Be real with yourself and give yourself grace. Everybody does stupid things at some point in their lives, and it's OK to admit it. In fact, it's preferable. You don't need to bottle up that shame and relive it; you can release it and move on.

Going forward, choose to avoid shame altogether. As a Boy Scout, I attended a leadership training where I learned the twelve principles of Scout law. Each principle was written on a lit-up sign that we walked past each night. "I'm going to be trustworthy," and "I'm going to be loyal," among others. We placed a pebble on top of each sign, a symbol of our decision to act on those principles in advance. If you weren't fortunate enough to learn similar principles as a child, you can still learn them now. It's never too late to protect yourself from shame.

Our youngest son just turned nine. He can decide now at this age that he's never going to try drugs. His choice at nine will govern his response to temptations for the rest of his life. The earlier you decide what you will do, the less likely shame will ever be a problem. Figure out what your principles are now, and stick to them when it matters most.

"Remember who you are and what you stand for," Cara and I remind our kids as we send them out the door each day. "Don't do anything we wouldn't do!"

We have explained many times that "we understand you're going to make mistakes. Try to make sure they're mistakes that can be cleaned up in a year or two." Of course we don't want them to make mistakes, but we're all human. Mistakes are part of life.

Joking aside, I know they understand. More times than I can count, Cara and I have had talks that went a little something like this: "We hope we've taught you enough that you won't compromise your principles, no matter what scenario you're in. If you stick to your principles, you'll never have anything to be ashamed of. You feel shame only when you compromise what you believe."

Treating Instant Gratification

Last June, I flew to Brazil and met with a company that wanted to partner with us. They manufacture industrial boats that apply chemicals in waterways. I knew going into that meeting that their offer would be hard for me personally to resist. Why? Because I'd feel like a kid in a toy store. I *love* boats. Always have. How could I say no to being part owner of a fleet?

Well, I did. I stuck with the fundamentals. I turned down buying the marine company. I simply asked myself, *Is this the right play at the right time?* It wasn't. We'd be in a lose-win scenario, risking our money without any safeguards around our investment. I then remembered what the feeling of instant gratification never tells you—not now doesn't mean never.

"I'm interested," I told the boating company CEO. "But not right now. We're going to wait. It wouldn't benefit us at this point."

These are hard words to say in business. I wanted a deal, but I knew it fed only a temporary desire for instant gratification. Saying no to something you want is beyond tough.

Months later, the CEO called me with an updated offer.

"Other segments of our business have grown so much now that we can't manage it alone," he said. "What if you joined with us without investing anything up front? Would you become a partner and manage the company for us?"

"That's more than doable," I said. "A win-win."

I delayed gratification, and it pays off as we execute on what we do best and allow the partner to do what they do best. Understanding what you want down the road lets you sidestep instant gratification. If we stop and think, and remove ourselves for some uninterrupted clear thinking, the emotion fades away—or at a minimum, we're able to keep it in check.

ATS recently finished a safety shower equipment contract with the federal government. I felt tempted to add an extra deliverable for an easy upsell, but one of our customers sells that same equipment. That would put us in direct competition with a potential marquee customer. What's an executive to do? I weighed my options. Make extra revenue in the short term but lose a good customer in the long term? Or do the exact opposite? Instant gratification lost that battle. I felt tempted to go for the quick money but knew maintaining a customer relationship was the better judgment.

More money, more opportunities, and more pleasure aren't the only forms that instant gratification takes. Have you ever felt a sense of urgency, the feeling that you have to act right now to relieve the pressure? "Oh no, Chase quit! We need to replace him! We better hire someone this week!" Chances are the person you hire to plug the hole won't be a good long-standing decision. Panic forces bad decisions. Resist the urge to find an instant fix. Sometimes your best decision is the decision to postpone it. Not everything needs to be resolved immediately. Counterintuitive in our clickbait world, I know. We want it now, we get it, repeat. Decisions that have weight or value—like those in water treatment—need to be thought through.

Slowly . . .

I recently bought a golf audiobook to help me improve my golf swing. The introduction advises golfers of all ages and skill levels to practice every part of the swing in slow motion. Slow swings increase the speed at which your muscle memory learns how to hit perfect golf shots without thinking about it. The same applies to decisions.

Sometimes it helps to slow down our decision-making, then slow it down even more. How slow? When longtime General Motors president, chairman, and CEO Alfred P. Sloan would make an important decision, he waited three weeks before formally revisiting the decision. Then he would review all the information again to see if he still agreed with his initial decision. Then he'd repeat the process, waiting three weeks more, and repeat the process *again*. Do you agree with yourself three out of three times? If yes, it's probably a good decision.

Slowing down is one of the hardest things you'll ever do, whether you're resisting instant gratification or relieving pressure in urgent situations. But if you slow down and think it through, you'll save time, energy, and probably heartache that would've gone toward undoing the wrong decision. The next time you step into a clear stream, wait for the cloud to settle so that you can move faster than you ever have before.

CHAPTER 7

The Fundamentals of

Uncompromised Decision-Making

"I Don't Have a Choice."

We've all said this at one point in our lives. Faced with a difficult decision, we wanted to do the right thing. Yet surrounding circumstances made the right decision feel impersonal, impractical, or impossible.

Maybe you hired an employee you thought was a superstar in the making, but it's become clear that you can't count on them to show up on time. *Now what?* Perhaps you promised your teenager you'd leave work early to attend their big performance. Then your boss assigned you a project to finish before 8:00 a.m. the next day. *Now what?* Or maybe you worked on a deal that roped in so many decision-makers in your company and your client's company that you couldn't reach a consensus. *Now what?*

In most situations where you feel tempted to compromise, there *is* a way forward. Even in the highest pressure scenarios, you can do the right thing without sacrificing your integrity or the outcome you want. These treatments may not be obvious, but I promise you—they're there. They've been revealed to me throughout my career, and now I'd like to share them with you.

Treating Subjective Experience

Have you ever achieved a positive result but had no idea *how* you did it? You bought into a mutual fund that became the top performer of the year. Your kids' best behavior during church earned you a compliment from the elderly couple everyone respects. Thirty minutes after you rolled out the new company website, a prospect filled out your contact form. What can you learn from these successes? Nothing, unfortunately. Success is a poor teacher. If we reflect on a positive outcome in hopes of recreating it in the future, all we'll find is the painful definition of "one-hit wonder." Here's how it goes. Let's say a tech entrepreneur starts their first software company. In short order, their business takes off. Everyone calls the entrepreneur a prodigy. This entrepreneur then goes around acting like they can do everything. By accident or by luck, they started their first venture in the right industry at the right time. But when they build their next venture the same way as their first, the business fails. The circumstances that worked for one formula do not always transfer to a new set of circumstances.

We have a saying at ATS. "Strategically forget the past." Our subjective experience doesn't tell us a whole lot about making wise decisions in new situations. To keep our own success from misleading us, we borrow knowledge from other industries and people. For example, we look at advances in software, smart sensors, and mobile apps and ask, "How could we apply these to the low-tech water treatment industry?"

Recently, ATS has leveraged artificial intelligence to introduce smart water systems software that can prescribe and predict future water quality, pump efficiencies, and maintenance needs. In the meantime, our competitors still advertise in paper catalogs. As the older crop of people running water plants retire, we need millennials to step up and take their place. Engineers in their twenties and thirties don't want to work with tech from the 1960s. They want to control everything in work and in life from their smartphones or laptops. Providing smart systems gives them that control. Keeping your eye open to developments in other industries can help you stay ahead of the competition.

Any time you go from one industry to another, you can borrow and reuse best practices. This is called transference. Reapplication of proven methods helps companies and people succeed. You can do this by studying other industries. How are they dealing with the unfamiliar situation you're facing? Most brilliant inventions are old ideas put to a different use. Have you ever seen a watercraft propeller? Maybe you steered a rowboat using an inboard motor and propeller or visited a museum where a ship with its giant propeller was displayed?

The origin of the screw propeller starts with Archimedes, who so famously used a screw to lift water for irrigation and bailing boats that it became known as the Archimedes screw.[47] Shipbuilders got the idea for modern propeller design from agriculture. Devices called corkscrews move water through an irrigation canal from lower levels to higher where the crops are. One day a corkscrew broke, a farmer repurposed the device for his rowboat, and the rest is transference history. As the official story goes, in 1785 in England, Joseph Bramah proposed a propeller solution of a rod going through the underwater aft of a boat attached to a bladed propeller, though he never built it. About twenty years later, Edward Shorter proposed using a similar propeller attached to a rod angled down that temporarily deployed from the deck above the waterline, thus requiring no water seal and intended only to assist becalmed sailing vessels. He tested it on the transport ship *Doncaster* in Gibraltar and at Malta, achieving a speed of 1.5 mph (2.4 km/h).

Transference isn't the only way you can approach a major decision with fresh insights. Learn from the people in your life who make

---

[47] "Lift Water with an Archimedes Screw," Ben Finio, *Scientific American,* July 11, 2019, www.scientificamerican.com/article/lift-water-with-an-archimedes-screw.

principled decisions. One of my secrets to smart decisions in stressful situations is to first talk it through with my wife, Cara. She asks tough questions, is open-minded, and knows how to size people up. She's my truthful sounding board. She knows where my weak spots are, so she can get real with me and say, "That's really how you interpret/understand it?" You're never going to get that honesty from an employee (or an employer).

It was my father who taught me to discuss work issues with Cara. On anything my father thought was crucial, he would say to me, "I'm going to take this home and discuss it with your mother." He had a point. In my first business class in college, the textbook said that a CEO's success is often predicted by the strength of their marriage. Although that may not be the prevailing belief currently, it is true in more ways than can be discussed in this book.

A lot of employees have spouses who don't know anything about what they do at work. They know where they work, and that's about it. If your job requires you to make tough choices—and what job doesn't?— you must have somebody to talk to. You can't always talk to coworkers, management, or the company's board. You can talk to attorneys, but they bill you and often don't understand business.

In fact, there are certain things you can't talk to anybody about other than your spouse. For example, if you work at a publicly traded company and you tell your golf buddies about an upcoming deal, you could get yourself into legal trouble. Those golf friends could buy stock, and the Securities and Exchange Commission can subpoena your emails, texts, and calls for the last six months to see if you talked to anyone who made money. Some dilemmas need to be shared strategically and carefully, and having the right person as your sounding board makes all the difference when making critical decisions.

Getting your spouse's thoughts before you make a critical decision at your company may be the most profitable piece of advice you take away from this book. I once met an entrepreneur who was offered $500 million for the company he owned. He went home and took his wife for a drive so that they could discuss it. His wife helped him see past the dollar signs by reminding him that they had a goal together and that it was different from the current offer. They decided to turn it down. They knew their company value would only go up as they achieved their goal. They were well off enough, so there was no rush in selling then. As it turned out, their wait paid off. A few years later, they were offered several billion dollars for the purchase of their company, and they accepted and held fast to their shared goal.

If you don't have anyone to talk to but yourself, you tend to make bad decisions. It's easy to overanalyze risks, keeping yourself up at night stressing about work and robbing yourself of being present for your family or friends because of decisions that need to be talked through with someone. When you're able to talk decisions over with someone else—even if all that person does is listen—you can often reach some clarity.

If you're not married, seek advice from mentors. Don't have a mentor yet? Call a business leader in an industry who you're noncompetitive with (this way they won't feel like they're helping a competitor if they share advice). Reach out and ask, "I'd really like to pick your brain on something. Could I have an hour of your time? I'll take you to lunch." Most people are flattered if you ask for their opinion. Successful people love to help others become successful. They enjoy sharing their perspective and often have a lot to offer. These conversations sometimes turn into long-term mentoring relationships.

Of course, successful mentors won't have much free time, but if you execute the advice they give you, they'll want to help you again. When I ask my mentor a question, I apply his advice and then email him with the results. "Here's what transpired, here's what's happening, and here's my next question." I follow up and report back.

I met one of my mentors, Greg Butterfield (now an ATS board member), when I was sixteen years old. He was my church youth leader and a successful businessman. At the time, he was growing a company called WordPerfect. He's since taken five companies to $1 billion in sales, several to multimillion-dollar exits, and other companies to $100 million in exits. Greg has also helped hundreds achieve lifelong financial goals. He always makes sure his employees benefit when he sells a company, and he gives a substantial part of his income to support local charitable initiatives.

Is every mentor a role model like Greg? Not necessarily, and that's OK. In fact, you don't even have to know the person for their wisdom to have a positive effect on your situation. When you're facing a big decision and you're tempted to do the same thing as last time, head over to Amazon or visit your local library. Browse books on the topics you need advice about. I never met Peter Drucker, yet his counsel has helped me save multimillion-dollar deals and salvage relationships. Our lives are too short and limited to *not* learn from books and people. We can't develop enough personal experience in this lifetime to always know what the right decision is or what consequences to expect. That's why Warren Buffet reads five hundred pages a day.[48] He can't make decisions on his own any better than anyone else, so he looks at what other people have done for inspiration in his own decision-making.

The valuable takeaways from books aren't always the author's wins. Remember, everybody is self-made, but only the successful ones admit it. We don't hear about the wrong decisions that successful people made unless we dig into their stories. That's why books where authors share their failures are often the most valuable. The way I see it, you can learn only from your own mistakes, or you can read and also learn from other people's. "Wise men learn from the mistakes of others, fools from their own," I read once. Not every book has a direct application to your situation, but you can always ask yourself how their experience applies to yours. As my father-in-law always says, "Everything you need to know is already in someone else's head."

---

[48] "Berkshire Hathaway Star Followed Warren Buffett's Advice: Read 500 Pages a Day," Kathleen Elkins, CNBC, March 27, 2018, www.cnbc.com/2018/03/27/warren-buffetts-key-tip-for-success-read-500-pages-a-day.html.

Let's say you're facing a big decision right now. You've talked it over with your spouse or a mentor you respect (or both), but you're still on the fence. How do you know which authors to consult? I always do my homework to see if an author's real-life accomplishments are worth studying. Just because somebody wrote a *New York Times* best seller doesn't mean we should follow their advice. There are lots of sharp thinkers who've lived shady lives. For example, John F. Kennedy couldn't teach anything about marital fidelity, but you could learn political skills from his life's work.

If you're on the fence about a decision, step back and give attention to both sides. If you're afraid of reading more about the side you're not leaning toward, chances are you're missing an important perspective. Listen to both opinions about the decision and gather information. Get your research from a trustworthy source. For example, I would not look for reliable information on the Republican party from the Democrats' website. In politics and in life, there are good, smart people on both sides. Hold your judgment and consider an author's case. Cara and I recently read a book about Emma Smith, wife of the prophet Joseph Smith Jr. We took the time to look up each source quoted. It became clear that those who dislike him had only bad things to say. Those who saw the prophet Joseph as a prophet were in constant awe and respect for the good that Joseph and Emma did. It's tempting to rebut an argument in your head while you're reading it. Instead, try to consider what they have to say. It doesn't matter who they are or what position they hold. They have something to teach you if you're willing to learn.

Treating Too Many Decisions

What do you do when you're faced with more decisions than you can handle? The more snap judgments you make at once, the likelier they will *all* be the wrong ones. Feeling like you're in a lose-lose situation? Acknowledging that you're in over your head is your first step to handling it.

Second, narrow down your choices to a manageable number using the three solutions system. For each decision you have to make, there is a good way forward, an OK way, and a lousy way. Identify those three options for each decision with your spouse or mentor, in a spreadsheet, or on a whiteboard or piece of paper. Sometimes identifying the *worst* choice you could possibly make brings the right decision to light. On occasion there are two good decisions; however, they take you down different paths, so you better know where you want to end up.

Once you narrow down your possible choices for each decision, you'll relieve the feeling of being overwhelmed. You see, it's not the number of decisions that stresses us out but the worry over getting them all wrong and suffering the consequences. The three solutions system takes the pressure off so that you don't feel trapped by limitless options. It also creates a shortcut to the right decision while reducing the possibility of disaster to almost nothing.

Treating Pressure

"You need an answer right away? OK. I'll get it to you by the end of the day."

Ever made a promise like this to your clients, your boss, your children, or your spouse? You may not have had the information you needed by the end of the day, yet you gave your word anyway. How could you not? You know people are counting on you, and you don't want to let them down.

The person asking for your decision probably didn't have the expectations you have of yourself. Without realizing it, you created a high-pressure situation. The next time someone implies that they need your answer right away, take a moment. Ask yourself, *How much time do I actually need to think this through and make the best decision?* Then tell the person, "I want to give this decision my full attention. With everything already on my schedule, I think I can get you an answer in a week. Is that all right with you?"

Setting a date in the near future (but not too near) gives you enough time to evaluate your options. Once you set expectations for yourself and the other person, the pressure is eased. Meeting those expectations requires some planning. I recommend a calendar for everything in your life, both personal and professional. It can be a paper calendar or day planner or a calendar app like Google Calendar that you can access from all your devices. Plan and schedule all the tasks you need to do, mundane things included. When a client or employee asks for my undivided attention, I can look at my schedule. If a time slot is taken, I say, "I've already booked something for this time. I know you're in a rush, so here's where my next opening is. Does that work for you?" Most of the time, people are OK with that. They're happy to have their own time on my schedule, even if it takes a little while to get to it.

That said, circumstances will arise when you'll need to be flexible. What if there's an emergency at home? What if a situation at work escalates and you find yourself in the heat of a battle for your future? There will be times when you cannot push a decision back several days. When that happens, how do you keep urgency from forcing you into a decision you'll regret? We can borrow a strategy from the military. In war, the military doesn't send the generals to the frontline to call the shots. It's not because they're afraid—they've faced combat before. They step back from battle so that they can think straight, see the bigger picture, and outsmart the enemy. The United States Navy SEALs even have a saying that applies to decision-making. "Slow is smooth, smooth is fast." When time is of the essence, step away from the frontlines. You need a clear head and calm nerves. Maybe you won't be able to take three days to make a decision, but you can probably take three hours. Go out golfing. You may not even play golf, but course etiquette means that you have to put away your smartphone. No tech, only nature. Now you can think. An executive I know played tennis before he had to make a hard decision. He never picked up a tennis racquet until he turned sixty, but now he goes to the court to take a break from emails, phone calls, and meetings. Whatever your activity, you want to get away from the high pressure and tight deadlines. It takes practice and some maturity and discipline, but you can take time for anything that is not trained as a reflex (such as emergency maneuvering of a plane that is crashing). Only then can you ask yourself, *What am I missing? Is there something I couldn't see while I was in the thick of it?* Time away from the situation can help you reach the right answer.

If you are one of several decision-makers in a situation, you can use a technique I call peel the onion. This technique gets all involved on the same page while alleviating the pressure everyone is feeling. When you meet with your fellow decision-makers, start the meeting by asking them, "Is this the meeting where we come to a conclusion? Or is this the meeting where we discuss possible ideas so that we can think about it first?" When people know the purpose of a meeting, they present their ideas differently. Often if they feel like the point of a meeting is to come to a conclusion, they're going to dig into their opinions and push back against open dialogue. But if everyone knows you're discussing options and they don't expect a final decision, you can peel back the problem together and lay out all possible solutions. Chances are this low-pressure meeting will result in a unanimous or near-unanimous conclusion. Slow is smooth, smooth is fast—try to take your time making a decision, and you'll save time because you've made the right one.

Treating Excess

It's easy to say no to something when you don't have the means to get it. It's trickier to say no when you can afford things you may want. When we have excess, we feel entitled to splurge on what we don't need. Excess can get us in trouble because we stop feeling the need to conserve. We don't take the time to ask ourselves, *Do I need this? Would it enrich my life or others' lives? Is this diverting me from what I should be doing?* Most people experience excess in some form, whether it's a raise, a Christmas bonus, or just an extra day off. It's how we choose to use our excess that counts. We may start attending all the NBA games because we can afford box seats. Or we could write a check to the fundraising drive for our child's school library. We might collect muscle cars because why not? Or we could volunteer to pack meals at the food bank.

People I would consider truly successful who have excess money and time use it wisely. They don't let it change them. Maybe they splurge on a fresh-cut steak, a slightly nicer home and car, or maybe a bucket list vacation occasionally, but that's the biggest change in lifestyle.

In my faith, we're encouraged to be "anxiously engaged in a good cause" (Doctrine and Covenants 58:27–28). For me, this means staying busy doing good, which eliminates downtime that leads to mischief. Maybe for you that means sponsoring a sporting event for a good cause or reading your scriptures first thing each morning. In my experience, if

I put my energy into helping people, I don't have a lot of extra idle time, which lowers the opportunity to make poor decisions.

Treating No Follow-Through

For every miracle you hear about in the news, there are dozens of tragedies you don't.

To rescue the trapped miners in Chile, the federal, state, and local governments made a joint decision—*these people are going to live*. That decision changed the outlook of the situation. Decision-makers moved from "Can they be rescued?" to "How do we make this rescue happen?" The rescue was a once-in-a-lifetime victory for the Chilean nation. Lots of people from all over the world moved to help out. And it all started with the decision to save all thirty-three lives. When you decide the outcome you want in advance, you figure out how to get over every obstacle, just like the drilling teams did. If you, like the Chilean government, are willing to say, "I'll move everything I can to make this happen," you probably will.

Will you always succeed when you decide the outcome you want in advance? Not always. Is making the right decision as simple as putting your mind to it? Not quite. But approaching the dilemma with the decision to succeed no matter the obstacle helps and never hurts.

Treating Trends

Ever heard of Hasbro? If not, chances are you've seen or even bought Tonka trucks, Play-Doh, and Mr. Potato Head—all toys owned by Hasbro. Up through the 1970s, board game sales brought Hasbro consistent cash flow. What happened to change that? A new trend—both dad and mom began working outside the home. That meant they could afford to entertain their kids with new toys. Hasbro leadership looked to the future and saw video games, so they prepared to ride the trend. Smart move. Hasbro became the number three video game publisher within three years of its founding.

You can't literally see the future, so you're not going to get the trends right all the time. But if you're watching what's starting to change, *you* can change with the times. In water treatment, a recent trend right now is certified organic. It's deceptive. Some organic fruits and vegetables are produced the same way as the conventional versions of the same crop. If farmers tell consumers that their avocados are certified organic, they feel good about paying more. In reality, they're paying for that certification. Very often, conventionally grown avocados may have no more pesticides than their organic counterparts.

Another new trend is pitching in to meet the developing world's need for clean drinking water. Everybody in that space has the right motive. But as charities have provided clean water, too often they've built the sewer or septic tanks too close to drinking water. When nobody steps up to educate the locals about waterborne illness, what happens? Sewers run into the drinking water, causing the same sickness that brought clean water advocates over in the first place.

I've also noticed that many clean water advocates don't understand the need for clean farm water. People also need clean food to pair with that potable water. Yet across developing nations, millions of reservoirs, rivers, lakes, and streams remain contaminated. The water is unusable, even for crops. At ATS and Empower Mali, we saw past the trend and have offered people what they really needed. You might say that we're picking up where many trend-chasers leave off, building world-class sewers and septic tanks to keep drinking water pure.

Is it possible to ride a wave before it hits the shore? Yes. The founder of lululemon, a high-end activewear store frequented by millennials, agrees. His approach to trend-chasing is the rule of three. If he hears about an idea three times from different sources, he figures a trend is building. Several years before he started lululemon, three different people told him to try yoga. *Maybe yoga's a real trend, and maybe people need yoga pants.* It turned out that he was right.

Few companies make it with trends. Some water treatment products I've seen over the years make claims that don't follow science. Maybe it's a cool idea. Maybe they get featured in industry magazines. But they don't always take chemicals and physical laws into account. Thirty years ago, there was a trend to put a "brick" of treatment chemicals in the bottom of a cooling tower. Seems simple, right? Not so much. That water got saltier and saltier. Saltwater is corrosive, so the chemical-saturated water ended up creating scale as well as eating the cooling towers. Water treatment technicians should've known up front that that would happen. When you see a trend on the rise, do the research first and ask questions. *Does this make sense with what we've learned in the last fifty years? Why is it unique? Why would it work?*

Why wouldn't it work? Make sure a trend is here to stay. If not, your timing is going to be critical if you're going to make any money. Otherwise, you may lose money chasing it.

Treating C Players

If people are rowing your boat the wrong way, or not rowing at all, then get them off. If you don't, your A players will abandon ship first. Most leaders I meet feel like they can help their C players turn the corner. *It's too soon to fire them. They can still get it right.* I understand. It's hard to let somebody go. Your thoughts go to things like *What did I do to fail them? Why didn't they work out? What conditions did I set up? Did I undercut them? Was there something I did that made it so that they couldn't succeed? Do people think I'm a cold leader?*

Life is short. The clock ticks quickly. Being continually surrounded by C players may not be how you want to spend your work life. By letting them go, you're making it easy to find and keep A players. Your team will be stronger for having only strong people on it. More stuff gets done. It's easier to set and meet goals. Each person feels like they're carrying less of a load. You still work long hours, but you don't realize it because you're having fun changing the world together.

I have learned a great deal about the value of building a core team of A players in my company. One of the main things is that A players attract other A players. The best want to work with the best, so they refer the best. They won't ask me to interview anybody for an open position who isn't the best because they don't want to be dragging them around. But B players bring C players so that they look better. If an employee is not an A player, they don't want to work with one because they know that top performer will make them look unproductive or apathetic. An A player wants the best because they know everybody wins. It's a little like playing ball at a competitive level—it's totally different from a pickup game. People who are good like to play against other people who are good. Winners want to be on winning teams. Successful people like to work with other successful people.

How do you find A players to replace your Cs? Begin by finding people who share your same goals. Everybody on your team should understand what the endgame looks like and what it will take to get there. There should be complete transparency. That way, when someone isn't working out, your other employees won't look twice when you say goodbye. When people aren't aligned, they hoard information and hold private discussions with team favorites.

I try to look for curious, self-teaching A players who believe in the power of innovation. I've found a simple question to use in an interview to tell if the person I'm talking to fits my idea of an A player.

Richard: "Do you read much?"

Candidate: "Oh, I read tons."

R: "What was the last book you read?"

C: "Um . . . gosh, it was like six months ago. A novel, I think."

If someone can't tell me the last book they read, they probably have no curiosity. They're not a learner. What new discovery are they well informed on? Can they really define what changes are happening in the industry and why they are significant? They're a C player. No further questions needed.

For executive staff members, we look for people who've run a business before. If they haven't paid a business's bills and, more importantly, they haven't made a payroll, they're not going to be on the same page as the rest of the executive team. Somebody who's worked only for big companies with a flat growth curve and abundant cash makes different decisions from a leader who's building a growing company. I've brought people in from billion-dollar companies before, and it seemed they were out of their element. I expect quick changes. But usually when they come from a large corporation, they're used to taking six to eighteen months to make decisions that help move the company forward.

Just as high-growth businesses like ours are tight on time, we're also short on cash because we grow as fast as we can. Cash-rich companies can get by for a long time by throwing money at most problems that arise. Former business owners are careful and strategic with company funds. People who worked at $100+ million companies probably have milked the money for decades. By having people on our team who know what it's like to sweat through a payroll or to personally cover costs, we're more like-minded and more likely to succeed.

Another way I've found to ensure that candidates are a good fit with ATS is to start them on a part-time basis. When I hire someone without being able to see how they work, the likelihood of success is chancy. Having people do something for you first can pay off. For example, our operations guy worked for ATS for four months part time before I hired him full time with salary and benefits. By the time the contract period is over, you have a very good idea of what you're getting and how the person fits in culturally with the company.

When I first hired our CFO as an hourly consultant, he was working for another company. As a consultant, he set up a new employee expense management system to automate accurate expense reporting. I got to see the speed at which he executes and how he interacts with everyone—from interns to board members. "This guy is solid," people he worked with told me. After our trust in each other was established, I offered him a full-time job with ATS.

I've made similar part-time arrangements with our finance person, our marketing person, our graphic designer, and our content writer. I told our product management person, "I'll give you part ownership of the company if you produce revenue." Without paying him a penny up front, we gave him an opportunity to prove himself, which he did. When these relationships work out before employees come on board officially, everyone wins. Usually whenever I've transitioned people into my companies one step at a time, it's worked out. If you're looking for the lowest risk way to recruit and hire, this is it.

When you're recruiting and hiring A players, you might be surprised at what motivates them. Past a certain point, money is not the driver. Money doesn't keep people working for a business. A belief in a cause and feeling important at work are far more important. Whether their motivation limit is $60,000 or a $1 million net worth, everybody has a cap where more money doesn't pull them out of bed in the morning.

"I make more now than my dad ever made," an employee (an A player) told me after his annual raise.

"Is that so? How do you feel about that?"

"Well, my wife and I can support our kids, we have a home we love, and we get to go to the beach every summer." He chuckled. "So I'm set, for life!"

Financial security is important, but what about bonuses? Do companies use those to fire up their A players? I once read a study that found that 95 percent of financial incentives get paid out whether employees perform or not. It's company welfare. I approach bonuses differently.

First, to understand how to motivate your A players, take an interest in their interests. What do they want to accomplish in life? What are their life goals? Most people aren't working toward their number one goals. They give up what they want to do to make sure their mortgages are paid, their car payments clear, and their kids go to college. When you're young and just getting started, you get paid by the hour. It's nearly impossible to take a vacation when you must *pay* for the vacation by losing a week's paycheck while still needing to pay your bills on time.

I believe in having a system in place to make sure our employees know that we care about them, that they're part of a family. I choose to reward employees when they go above and beyond for the company. Maybe their lifelong goal is going back to school or taking an all-inclusive golf course vacation. I have tried to create a culture wherein if an employee works hard, ATS will pay for advanced courses. Do well in your position and we'll send you to your tee time. Why is it important that I pay for an employee's career development rather than just write a check? How is this different from the bonuses other companies give out? If he had earned a cash bonus, he'd feel selfish keeping it to himself rather than spending it on his family. The same with an employee's vacation reward. She'd take that money and buy something for her kids, not herself.

If you can find out what truly motivates your employees, you don't have to worry about offering huge salaries. The market sets what people should earn for their roles. Help your A players achieve what they want in life, and you'll keep them loyal and actively engaged in their work.

Treating Unfair Consequences

Life isn't fair. Neither is golf. If you've ever had a good walk spoiled, as Mark Twain referred to the sport, you know how a good round can go bad at no fault of your own. For example, I once drove my golf ball into the middle of the fairway. It landed wrong on a branch and careened off into the trees. What's my next shot? That first bit of bad luck wasn't my fault. My second shot could safely take my ball back onto the fairway, setting me up for a safe third shot to try to make par, or I could approach it like I'm Tiger Woods 2.0. I could aim for the green as close to the hole as possible. When it does not go well, my second shot traps me deeper into the forest. The shortcut never seems to work for me. In my experience, the shortest route to safety is to punch the ball a few yards, get it back into play, and make sure the next shot has a good setup.

It's the same when someone else's decision takes your life off course. When a broken promise, breach of trust, or just plain bad choice by another puts you in that situation, the worst thing you can do is give up in hopelessness. Don't convince yourself that the only chance you have is one miracle shot to fix everything at once. Get yourself out of the forest and back in the game.

In life, my punch shot is my personal creed. My creed is a set of statements about who I'm going to be in the future as a husband, a father, and a businessman. It's an intimate document that I don't share with many people. Some call it a mission statement. This one- to two-page document models how you want your life to turn out. What do you want to accomplish spiritually, personally, and professionally? Who do you want to become? The future is today. What I do today determines who I become.

If you sit down to create your own personal creed today, those unfair consequences will be a whole lot easier to overcome tomorrow. Everyone's going to end up in the trees at some point in their life. That's why everyone needs a creed now. It helps draw you toward making decisions in line with your ideal future. Whether you're in life's open fairway or you find yourself deep in the forest, your creed will help you decide. *No, that decision doesn't take me where I want to go.* And as you consistently make better decisions, even if you're around people who make poor ones, your creed puts you in a position to enjoy your journey.

When you set out to write your personal creed, envision how you want to live. Write down everything in detail. How do you want to grow? What is your financial ability and your financial goals? Where do you see yourself and your family? How are things around you at work, at church, and with friends? Write as if everything you want has already happened, and your mind will figure out how to get you where you want to be. The mind is an amazing and underused tool.

Treating Overstaying

In the early 2000s, telecommunications corporation WorldCom slid from scandal toward bankruptcy. I remember headlines about accounting fraud, inflated stock prices, and the CEO's resignation. When the big story broke that WorldCom leadership had lied about the company's total assets, their stock dropped toward zero. Every colleague who had money in WorldCom told me to throw my money in, too.

"Buy it! You'll get it at such a great price!"

I didn't buy. I had a feeling they were saying that because they wanted their own stock to work out so badly. There wasn't anything they could do about it, so they were sticking with it. But it was too late to dig out. They could have abandoned the stock and cut their losses when the scandal broke, but instead they held out for the stock to recover (it didn't).

We all have a WorldCom. Maybe yours is an investment, a career, or a relationship. We know the good times are long gone, but we feel that maybe, just maybe, if we dig deeper we'll find a ladder out. Understand what you want out of the situation. If you're not going to get what you want, leave. Easily said, I know, and not so easily done. It becomes easier as we make a habit out of it.

My father taught me how to leave when it's time. He wanted to be home from work every night at 5:30 to have dinner with the family. Every day at 4:45 p.m. he wrapped up his work. He quit for the day no later than 5:01. He often said, "That's enough fun for today! We'll start again in the morning." I rarely saw my father get taken by a bad investment scheme or get stuck in a bad business deal. I attribute that wisdom to his daily habits. Focus on the things that need to be done and train yourself to leave when it's time.

The next time you're faced with a difficult decision and you feel that you don't have a choice, remember that you always have a choice if you decide to see it. Whether you talk things over with your spouse, ask someone for more time to contemplate, or pass on a trend to show you can, smart decision-making will start to come naturally. After you make it through the rough patch, the next one you hit will feel easier to handle. And who knows? Maybe you'll start getting critical tasks done on time so that you can leave work at 5:01.

CHAPTER 8

The Fundamentals of Productive

Decision-Making

If Only Self-Help Helped

The self-help industry is worth $10 billion. Like me, you're probably part of the reason why. We've bought books, audiobooks, webinars, CDs, DVDs, and yes, VHS tapes to get motivated, feel inspired, and improve ourselves—so many that we think in success quotes:

- *Can't forget to pick up milk at the grocery on the way home from work. My family will forget what I said. They'll forget what I did. But they'll never forget if I come home without milk for breakfast.*

- *I wish my kids would just listen and obey me the first time. The allowance belongs to those who prepare for it today.*

- *If I hire a second assistant to catch up on client emails on weekends, I'll have a better chance of renewing more contracts. Everything I want is on the other side of an email.*

Famous sayings are fun when they align with what we already believe. Yet when I think about the thousands of hours of self-improvement content I've consumed over the years, most boils down to two little words.

"Try harder."

Add a heartwarming story, toss in a seven-step "get successful quick" system, slap a cover on it, and you've got yourself the next self-help best seller. Like me, you've probably come away from such books, articles, and seminars feeling frustrated with yourself. You're promised that if you put in the effort, you'll be able.

To overcome your negative tendencies, fix your attitude and get out of your own way for good. If only trying harder worked. Twenty-five years in water treatment has taught me why most self-improvement "tips" are as empty as the wallets of people who keep buying them. Unproductive traits, like a tendency to put off important decisions, come naturally. Simply trying your best to *not* procrastinate is like trying to solve a problem with a problem. It doesn't work. We don't add more chlorine to overchlorinated water in hopes of making it safer. That's not how nature—or human nature—works. Try putting off putting off and see how far that gets you.

In my experience, the best way to treat our destructive instincts is to create structures around our routines, our relationships, and ourselves. These structures keep us from making poor decisions that otherwise happen naturally. Finishing the proposal ahead of the deadline isn't all about pushing yourself to keep working. It's a matter of setting up your schedule so that postponing the task becomes impossible. The same goes for every unproductive trait, both the ones you've been trying to fix and those you've given up on.

Treating Overoptimism

Know Thy Strengths and Weaknesses

Before ATS hired our CFO, we hired and fired two executives who overestimated their abilities and underestimated the strengths required for the job.

"I don't like talking to bankers," the now ex-EVP of finance said. "It's intimidating."

As the EVP of finance, funding the company's growth is one of the most important parts of your job. If you don't like doing that, this isn't a good job for you. He didn't last long.

In another company, our new bookkeeper didn't understand how to enter transactions found on the company's balance sheet into our accounting software. She led us to believe that she did. But after a month on the job, she could no longer hide it. It became obvious that she didn't grasp Accounting 101.

"No, I'll try harder," she said when I called her into my office to discuss her future.

"Well, it's not something you can just 'try harder' at. You don't understand the principles of accounting. There are other jobs that could be a better fit for you, even within our company, but accounting isn't it. Why did you tell us that you knew what you were doing? Why haven't you asked for help on anything?"

She didn't answer. She resigned on the spot.

People who understand themselves and what they're good at (and what they're not) ask all kinds of questions. They're not afraid to ask questions because they know it helps get the end result they want. A lot of times, people are afraid to ask questions because they don't want to look stupid or incompetent. The opposite is true. Asking questions shows you're thinking through the process and figuring out where the holes are. The ability to ask the right questions is one of the most important skills we can acquire in life. The right questions lead to truth.

I assume neither of these employees asked for help because they worried they'd be perceived as weak. Nobody likes to admit their weaknesses, especially when money is involved. But how much more fulfilling would work and life be if we were honest about them? Imagine how different those executives' career paths at ATS would've been if they'd discussed with me their actual strengths and weaknesses.

Stick with Your Strengths, and Let Others Stick with Theirs

I know what I do well as a leader in my company. I'm good at listening to people, seeing the big picture, being persistent, and dealing with complex and high levels of ambiguity. I'm good at seeing around obstacles that stop others from moving forward. I'm not good with details. So I focus on my strengths. Where I'm not the best, I delegate and allow other people around me to step into the roles where they excel. When everyone works in their strengths, they thrive and the company thrives. That's true for me, for you, and for visionaries like Steve Jobs. You may think Jobs was the smartest guy in the world. Even Steve Jobs, as spectacular he was, always had other people running certain operations at Apple. When you harness the labor of fifty thousand engineers all working in their strengths, you look pretty darn smart!

True leaders realize they may be the smartest person at one, two, or even three things. I learned this when I was working on my master's degree. In one of my classes, the professor gave us group projects. Our first assignment was to justify free public transportation in Park City, Utah. As a fiscal conservative, I couldn't see the sense in the idea. The other two students in my group—a liberal Democrat and a Green Party progressive—didn't agree with my thinking. Yet as I interacted with them, I could see that these were smart men. They simply saw the transportation issue differently than I did. Together, we found a way to complete the assignment without compromising our principles. We put our strong ideas together, set aside our weak beliefs, and earned an A+ on the project. From this assignment I learned how to work with people of completely different ideologies.

I've carried that willingness to set aside ego for the greater good into water treatment. I know I'm not a detail-oriented guy. I don't mind ambiguity. When I glance at the newspaper, I read the headlines and a couple of key words. But ambiguity doesn't work in water treatment. We must work out the details. People need more feedback than "We'll figure something out," so I surround myself with people who thrive on details. Good data can help make sure we focus on the right thing.

Added to my list of strengths I'll never have is extroversion. I'm not someone who wants to dominate a conversation. But I can listen to people, understand another person's position, and evaluate situations well. When I go to key client meetings, I take an executive with me who's a talker so that they can discuss the client's thoughts and help get our point across. I focus on listening so that I can understand what the client's real needs are. Then we can have a meaningful conversation followed by a real solution.

Companies, teams, and families function best when everyone does what they do best. One of my executives hates talking to groups. You get more than ten people in a meeting, and he freezes. But one on one, he'll talk to anybody anywhere. Interpersonal communication is his strength. He remembers the names of everyone he's ever met and almost everything they ever said—as long as it's not in a group.

Yes, you could work on improving your weaknesses a bit. We should all learn and grow, but for the most part, we have to focus on growing within our strengths. Our talents are God given. As I'm building ATS, I ask myself, *How do I stay relevant? If I'm not growing, if I'm not learning, if I'm not trying to figure things out at a faster pace, then I'm not relevant.* The same goes for anyone in any role. If you're wasting time by focusing all your attention on your weaknesses, you're not building your strengths and you could fall behind. I see this all the time as new start-ups begin to grow. The entrepreneur takes on all tasks inside the business because he believes in the product, has the dream, and makes the contacts. But he's not capable of running the company by himself anymore. He may be able to wing it alone at first, but not once the business has outgrown his strengths. Imagine how great his company would be if he assessed his abilities and allowed others to work in their strengths for him and the growth of his dream. Yes, you can muscle through many challenges as you grow. It's in an entrepreneur's nature to push through. But survival mode isn't sustainable. That's not growth. Frankly, that's why most businesses don't scale. Only about 0.22 percent of start-ups ever make it to the middle market (annual revenue between $100 million and $250 million).[49] That's why, as your company grows, you need to bring in outsiders who have done things before that you haven't. People whose strengths are your weaknesses. It's not that they're smarter than you (although I find they often are), it's that they have experience and strengths in areas you don't. You don't know what a mountain looks like

---

[49] "Sizing the Market for US B2B Companies in 7 Charts," Shailesh, *Insights* (blog), July 13, 2016, www.compile.com/blog/insights/sizing-us-b2b-market-7-charts.

from the top until you get there. If someone else could *tell* you what it looked like, why wouldn't you listen?

Systems Overcome Weaknesses

Some things you must do as the leader—even if you don't feel you're good at them. But you *can* put systems and processes in place that force you to do them well. For example, I hold one-on-one meetings with my executives to make sure they've got a grasp of the details of their stewardship. At the end of the year, I schedule all those meetings for the upcoming twelve months. Just because I'm no good at details doesn't mean I can forget about them. I still have to make sure they're reviewed by the right people. I've also developed forms to track certain details I'd otherwise overlook. To help create these forms, I sat down with my mentor Greg Butterfield. Together, we took the time to think through ways for me to be the most productive and effective. That's one of the hardest parts of business—taking the time to think things through. It's easy to execute on most things that you have complete control of, but can you take the time to stop and think things through? The time necessary to ponder and really get it right? It requires a lot of energy and headache. Most people don't even know where to start. And most of us haven't engaged our mental capacity with the rigor that is needed since our college days.

Greg knew this. He helped me map out how and when to meet with executives, how long the meetings should take, and so forth. He wrote up a strategy completely different from anything I came up with. But it works.

Greg's strength benefits my team and me and makes work a whole lot more fun.

Take a moment to ask yourself, *Which parts of business do I enjoy or do better than anybody else? Is there an aspect of business I am drawn to?* I can usually see when people are in the wrong place. If they're not drawn to their assigned work, then they will always have an invisible barrier in the way of their success, and nothing seems to inspire them. If you feel like you do something better than anybody else and you enjoy it, that's probably what you're supposed to be doing. And what about the stuff you're putting off? Those are probably things that you're not very good at and that don't fulfill you.

Protecting yourself from overoptimism about your own strengths comes down a real gut check as to what your real strengths are and then working to improve those strengths while delegating areas you know are your weaknesses. If you put these strategies to use, you'll never have to read about "trying harder" again.

Treating Procrastination

The Immediacy Advantage

I suffered from mañana syndrome for many years. *Oh, I'm going to start that tomorrow. I'll make that phone call later. I don't have to do it right now.*

Then I saw successful people like my father and my father-in-law react fast when things needed to happen. I learned that if I needed to make something happen, I needed to act on it right now. The longer we wait, the easier it is to talk ourselves out of it.

This could be embarrassing. This could be uncomfortable. I'm not sure what to say. I'm not sure what they'll think of me. We get ahead in life by doing the uncomfortable things more often to achieve our goals.

Once you figure out what needs to be done, go do it. It doesn't matter how you feel or what people think of you. In the end, all that matters is getting it done. While everyone else is putting off important tasks, you can leap ahead of them because you're not afraid to get moving.

Return, Report, Repeat

In the Church of Jesus Christ of Latter-day Saints, we have a principle called return and report. When you have an assignment, you get started right away and get it done and then you return and report that the assignment was completed. Return and report is proactive, not reactive. When you get things done and report your results before asked, you eliminate tension and stress as well as keep communication clear.

Return and report helps companies be more successful. If employees get their work done and report their progress, everything runs smoother. But without return and report, natural procrastinators put off tasks, wait until they're pinned down, and then only provide half or vague answers. It's up to their superior to have a talk with them about their productivity or (if things don't improve) dismiss them. I don't want to have that uncomfortable conversation—no one does.

It's not only employees who return and report to management but also for management to report to the board and to be accountable to the subordinates—the principle goes both ways. We all perform better when we have to be accountable for our actions. If managers evaluate employees' performance regularly, they're doing employees a favor by letting them know where they stand in the company. It gives more cohesion between managers and employees. Put off these crucial conversations, and you increase the chances of somebody not doing their job well.

The easiest way I've found to work return and report into company culture is to introduce the principle at a meeting. Too often meetings turn into housekeeping—comparing calendars and sharing trivial information. Managers tick off a dozen little problems one by one and feel good about themselves. Meanwhile, employees' eyes glaze over or they feel ganged up on or they get back to their cubicles and don't remember a single thing discussed. Everybody's time got wasted because nobody returned and reported.

We can fix these problems. As you conclude a meeting, give specific assignments to specific people, who are responsible for reporting back by a deadline for completion. For example, a CEO could say, "Tim, here's the assignment we need you to do. Ron is project lead, so report back to him by this date and time. Contact Ron if you need any help."

It's now Tim's job to complete the task and report back to Ron by a certain date and time. Instead of Ron asking, "Did you get to that, Tim? Have you followed up?," Tim gets it done, reports to Ron, and shares the results. Tim's report can be an email or an in-person meeting. With return and report, nobody is waiting until next month's staff meeting to hear Tim say, "Well, I haven't got to it yet. But I'm thinking about it."

When an employee isn't returning and reporting, the problem could be one of two things: either they don't understand the assignment or they haven't bought into the principle. It's OK to take the time to teach somebody, but if you get to the point where they can't grasp the concept or refuse to return and report, you need to part ways. Stalling indicates that they are unwilling or underperforming. It's never fun to let somebody go, but if you don't, you'll lose the confidence of all the people who are willing and performing.

Return and report is also crucial in a volunteer setting like nonprofits or churches. When nobody's getting paid, it feels awkward to ask, "Hey, did you get that done?" People get defensive when there's no paycheck driving them or contract binding them. With return and report, most volunteers will take initiative, get things done, and report back when they're finished (or when they need help). A culture where information is pushed instead of pulled or needed to be compelled tends to be a happier environment.

Write, Track, Improve

Another strategy I've learned to avoid procrastination is to write down decisions, activities, and goals and then to track them.

Tracking the decisions you make and what comes of them helps speed up future decisions. By tracking our decisions, we can evaluate what happened and see if the outcome we hoped for came to pass. Over time, tracking decisions helps create predictable results. Tracking decisions also helps us learn from our failures. *What didn't work? Why didn't it work?* When you track a decision, you can learn from any failure once rather than repeat the same mistake over and over.

Recall that the average person makes thirty-five thousand decisions a day. You can't track all of them. If you can make a decision now, execute right away. It's called the immediacy advantage. The sooner you act, the more likely you'll achieve your desired results. That said, if a decision is going to take some time to carry out, maybe six months, a year, or longer, write down and track that decision. An electrical engineering CEO I know wins projects that take ten years, and he doesn't want to screw them up. With long-term projects, you've got to get all your teams on the same timeline and keep them there. The best way to succeed is tracking decisions and progress, then adjusting as needed. Remember, projects don't go bad—they start bad.

At ATS, we track executive decisions and long-term projects using Gantt smartsheets. A Gantt sheet is a bar chart that illustrates a project schedule, showing all activities from start to finish as well as the duration of each task.

Our executive vice president of marketing at ATS, Stephen, will plug anything I ask his team to do into his Gantt smartsheets. He can tell me exactly how much time it's going to take after accounting for the schedules of all the people who will touch the project. "The graphic designer will get this task done in three hours," Steve tells me. This keeps everyone on track with realistic expectations.

Another benefit of Gantt smartsheets is the ability to track productivity, not just decisions. For example, our employees track their time on tasks, and those numbers show up in the smartsheets. As employees map their time throughout the year, it begins to show a pattern of how time is really being allocated. I'm always surprised by how much time is wasted. It's a great way to find holes in your processes. Maybe a task wasn't communicated clearly the first time or the new hire didn't get trained correctly or an employee got an answer from the wrong person. Somebody has to spend time putting out all these little fires. There is a misconception that to make progress, you have to resolve a certain number of issues every day. You might have even caused some of them, but hey, you resolved several. You're only truly productive when you get the right things done each day.

Email is often the culprit of misuse of time. So much time is wasted when the wrong people get copied on emails. *Let's expand the group so that I feel more important. My fire's bigger and needs more attention than anybody else's.* People can't be productive when they're responding to time-wasting emails. It's so easy to respond to emails that don't deserve our attention—or at least not our immediate attention. Before you know it, an hour is gone.

It's easy to get caught up in just seeing how the day plays out, but then we don't do any of the important things. We get so bogged down in meetings and day-to-day activities. We go through the motions of getting things done and so we feel good about it, but we didn't do the important things. Why is that? Most people know what's important. But there's a tendency to procrastinate the yucky thing, the big task that's uncomfortable and isn't fun to do. So we find other things to keep ourselves busy that *feel* worthwhile. We often perceive tasks as beneficial that aren't. *I'm doing something, so I'm being productive.* We're not being productive unless we're moving toward our goal. Anything you're doing that's not moving you toward that goal is not productive. It's a time sucker. *But I'm busy. I've been on the phone all day and I've been sending email replies.* Yeah, some of those you shouldn't have responded to. That's why many executives have their calls screened. It's hard to get to them, and call centers hate it, but they're the most successful people you'll ever not talk to.

I've found a simple way to get important things done every day. Every morning I write down the three most important things that need to happen that day on a virtual note card. I keep that with me, and I get those tasks done. *If it doesn't fit on the card, it's not that important,* I tell myself. *If you get these things done before you go to bed, Richard, you won.* When we commit something in writing, we either see it as truly essential or we realize that nothing bad happens if we don't get it done. Only the essentials go on the note card.

Writing out what you want to get done shouldn't be exclusive to business. Many people experience a midlife crisis because they never wrote down their dreams for life. They wake up and realize they're not living out their dreams. You've got to plan your dreams and get people to hold you accountable to them. If it's your little secret, it may never happen.

Remember my creed? Every quarter I update and fine-tune that creed. I review the list of what I want to accomplish with my kids, family, and church. Initially, it was difficult to commit to paper. However, after so many reviews, it's now mostly just fine-tuning and providing better clarity. I have my wife proofread it so that she's aware of my goals. I send a copy to my mentors so that they can hold me accountable and make sure I follow through.

It can be hard to live your dream. Life is difficult at best, and everybody has an occasional crisis. It helps if you decide what you're going to do and then plan as thoroughly and clearly as possible how you're going to get there. Whatever you envision, write it down and plan for it. Whatever it takes. Take inspiration from my neighbor, a past president of Lincoln Financial. Forty years ago, he decided that if he accomplishes his goals during the week, he goes golfing on Friday. Even though he had to fight the obstacle of dyslexia, which slowed his ability to read well, he found a way. His first day in management, he hired four students to read reports to him so that he always had the information he needed to make the right decisions.

He never missed a Friday tee time.

Treating Assumptions

The Way Things Are

In our current world, it seems that truth doesn't matter anymore. We see opinions replacing facts in politics, in culture, and in business. Fewer and fewer leaders seem to stick with data to address issues. If a report violates our assumptions, we throw it out. We assume that the people conducting the study let their bias skew the results.

In water treatment, this thinking is deadly. The people running Flint, Michigan, assumed that their new, cheaper water pipeline would turn out OK. The facts suggested otherwise. Nobody in city leadership was willing to say, "Clean water is clean water. These are the facts about what it's required to have in it." Instead of speaking the truth, everybody tried to pin the blame. They avoided the real issues so that they could maneuver politically and avoid negative repercussions. The reality is that Flint could happen in any of three hundred major US cities as well as other drinking water sources in the world. Somebody loses track of the basics, runs with their assumptions, and contaminates crucial water supplies.

My father founded our company on integrity. He would always say things the way they were. Plant managers, engineers, and politicians trusted what he said because he spoke the truth, whether it was good or bad for him. His reputation held up inside the company as well. He created an environment where anyone could speak the truth without worrying about retribution. Like my father, I'm aware that I don't know everything. That means that I've found people who fill my knowledge gaps and call me out when I'm making an unfounded assumption. I don't wait for this kind of feedback—I go get it. I regularly sit down with my team and get their evaluation. Not every suggestion is a good one, of course—as a leader, I still have to exercise wisdom—but I listen to anyone who wants to be heard.

Beware Enthusiasm

Jim Collins's book *How the Mighty Fall* looks at companies that quit doing what made them successful.[50] In every case, these companies changed direction and pursued new goals that weren't in the best interests of the company. I'm sure everyone was enthusiastic about the new direction, and the leadership either didn't recognize the shift or knew better but let employee enthusiasm dictate decisions anyway.

As a leader, you can accomplish three goals so that you never have to worry about this. One, assemble a team of A players. Two, make sure everyone knows where you're going. And three, tell everyone what the plan is to get there. Feedback and enthusiasm for change can be a good thing. Where companies get hurt is if enthusiasm is not in line with these three goals. After you've heard your team out, ask, "How do these ideas

---

[50] Jim Collins, *How the Mighty Fall: And Why Some Companies Never Give In* (New York: CLBusiness, 2011).

fit into our long-term goals? Do they still align with what we're doing?" If not, they're not in the company's best interests.

One Important Exception

In business and at home, there is only one safe assumption—that you don't have all the answers. Expect your employees to know things you don't. The same goes for your children. For example, your kid may be excited about a party that you think they shouldn't go to. It's easy to stomp out their desire to go, but hear them out first. Suspend your judgment. Don't share your opinion until they're done talking. Learn the facts first; how you feel about your children can cloud your judgment. Once you know the situation, you can share what you believe to be the right choice, give the moral reason why, and suggest an alternative if necessary.

Treating Overgiving

When Help Hurts You . . .

All too often we overgive when we want to make other people happy. We don't take into consideration what we want or need. Like most people, when I moved out of my parents' house, I still tried to please them despite having my own life, spouse, and career. It took some time to mature and to shift the allegiance to my immediate and growing family.

It's no different in business. I sat next to a gentleman from South Korea on a flight to Brazil to visit clients. Like everyone in business class, we made small talk to pass the time.

"I *hate* emails so much," he said as he opened the inbox on his tablet. "That's how everybody passes their workload off to me, day and night."

I nodded politely and gave a throwaway response. *If you hate it, why are you accepting the situation?* I thought. *You've let yourself get pulled into giving more of your time and your talents than you wanted. It's time to do something about it.*

All this gentleman needed was a boundary around his schedule. He could've set up an automatic out-of-office reply, for example. Anyone emailing him after 5:00 p.m. local time would get an instant response letting them know they will receive an answer during business hours.

We teach people how to treat us. Appropriate boundaries prevent people from walking all over you. These boundaries will keep you from hating others and yourself.

. . . and Others

I'm a proponent of charitable giving and serving the less fortunate. It is also important to think about the best interests of everyone in our network. It doesn't do any good to overcompensate employees. In fact, it does damage. I see it all the time with large severances when employees get fired or laid off. A severance pay an employee can live off for a year can be a career killer. By the time the money's gone, they may have forgotten how to interview or how to put in a productive day's work.

Whether you tend to be overgiving with coworkers, employees, or children, ask yourself, *Am I actually helping them, or am I trying to ease my conscience?* If it's the former, give to your heart's content. If it's the latter, withholding your time, talents, and treasure may be the most generous thing you can do. Learning to say no can help you avoid one of the most costly giveaways, which is your time. Be mindful of how it is used and with whom you share it.

Treating Self-Centeredness

The Power of Stewardship

People act entitled when they think they deserve more. Often if they don't get it, they think everybody's out to get them. One of the cures to entitlement is self-sufficiency. Self-sufficiency means that you can take care of yourself and provide for your family. I know I need to provide for my wife and kids so that we don't rely on other people to meet our needs. That keeps us from feeling entitled to something we don't deserve. Another cure for entitlement is humility. Remaining humble enough to learn from others helps them feel good by helping us and reminds us that we are not better than anyone else.

As a CEO, I try to use humility and self-sufficiency to take care of everybody in my stewardship. This may include such things as understanding employees' goals. For example, I want to make sure my operations manager feels self-sufficient. For him, that's making sure his whole team has what they need to get stuff done and also that they're paid fairly. I frequently evaluate myself by asking, "How do I make sure my executive team is properly cared for but also that revenue is flowing to everybody else in the company? Are we paying fair wages? Are we giving people opportunities to grow? Are we making sure everybody's needs are provided for as far as personal development and education? Do they have time off to spend with family? Can they get away if there's a health crisis and trust their colleagues to cover their work? Does everyone feel like they're safe in their work environment?" Because we've taken the time to address these questions and put systems in place to answer them, we hope to reduce the plague of entitlement.

No matter what problem you're facing, chances are there is at least one system to fix it. For example, building a culture of stewardship is a system, but it's not the only system. To teach people to take care of themselves, you can hold yourself to high standards. You can consistently speak the truth in love. These, too, are systems. As are those smartsheets. You can probably come up with a system of your own.

The point of any system is structure—stable attitudes and predictable behavior. It's the same in water treatment. Without stable testing methods and predictable technology, we wouldn't be able to control our clean water systems, much less clean the water itself. Is the water coming out of your tap always 100 percent pure? No, but it doesn't need to be in order to quench your thirst without harming your body.

Will this chapter's negative trait treatments work all the time for everyone? No, they won't. But they *will* work *most* of the time. Over the course of your life, that means more productive decisions and fewer unwise ones.

CHAPTER 9

Always a Choice

Pioneers, Agency, and the Last Bad Decision You'll Ever Make

Everybody deals with challenges, trials, setbacks, or family turmoil. Even if it doesn't appear that way on social media. A tough break. The loss of a spouse or child. Missed opportunities. Then there are the complicated emotions, difficult situations, and stubborn traits you have to work through to find your way to a new normal.

In this book I've offered practical lessons to help you deal with the most common causes of poor decisions. Ultimately, how you choose to put these lessons to use is your responsibility. Even in circumstances outside your control, you still have agency to act for yourself—the right to choose what you *do* next, even if you can't influence what *happens* next. Sometimes you'll be satisfied with the outcome, and sometimes you won't.

It's easy to blame others for things outside our control. There are some things we can't change about ourselves, and we sure as heck can't change what's happened to us. But we *can* decide what we're going to do next. As I went through my divorce, I chose to not become angry, bitter, resentful, and untrusting. I had my agency, and I used it to my advantage. I told myself on more than one occasion, *I have the ability to choose. I am going to be happy. I am going to make something out of my life. I'm not going to let this destroy me. This doesn't define who I am or who I become. This is not going to ruin God's plan of happiness for me.* Instead, I decided that I would learn from the experience, try to improve myself, and trust that God has good things in store for me.

I see lots of people who become bitter, angry victims for decades. You don't have to do that. No matter what life throws at you, you always have a choice to rise above and take a positive outlook. Awareness of your own agency, even when bad things happen to you, can be empowering. As the founding fathers of the United States wrote, God gave us unalienable rights, including the right to choose our decisions, behaviors, or reactions. Once you're aware of that, you can make better, growth-fostering choices.

As I look back on my own life, I realize that my close family and my mentors in water treatment taught me this from a young age.

To purify water, you remove the pollutants. Decisions, by and large, are the same way. Once you remove contaminants from your decision-making process, you tend to make smarter decisions. Water treatment is an ongoing process, as is sticking with a decision you've made. Once you've made what you believe to be the right choice, the hard part is over. The only wrong decision you can make at that point is to second-guess it and backtrack.

·I recently finished reading the book *The Hard Thing about Hard Things*.[51] Author Ben Horowitz asked Silicon Valley's most respected and experienced CEOs what the one thing was that made the difference between their failure and their success. For most executives, that one thing was the decision to see it through (whatever "it" was) and to never give up no matter what.

When you study people who have survived a harsh ordeal, you learn that they have one thing in common—they decided they were going to make it. They chose their outcome and then figured out how to achieve it. Look at the 1840s and 1850s Latter-day Saint handcart pioneers. These immigrants came to the United States from as far away as England, Sweden, and Norway. They chose to make the dangerous migration across mountains, deserts, and every biome in between to reach the Salt Lake Valley in Utah. They pulled handcarts packed with belongings,

---

[51] Ben Horowitz, *The Hard Thing about Hard Things: Building a Business When There Are no Easy Answers* (New York: HarperBusiness, 2014).

children, hopes, and dreams through rivers, sand, and snow. Not everyone made it. Those who did blamed no one. In fact, they were grateful for their experiences. They choose to be happy in their new life, they pressed on, and they endured to the end.

My great-grandfather was one of them. Together with 378 souls, sixty-one-year-old Isaac Allred departed Council Bluffs, Nebraska, on July 5, 1849, and set out westward. The Allred party totaled seventeen people—Isaac and his wife, Mary, and their children and grandchildren. A walk through the harshest lands of America wasn't the first or the last of their hard times. Almost twenty years prior, Isaac's son Reddick recorded what happened when the Church of Jesus Christ missionaries arrived at the Allred settlement.

My parents [Isaac and Mary] were members of a school of Presbyterians and brought up their children to reverence a God and were very exemplary in their lives, so that when a new religion was introduced they naturally looked at it with suspicion, having been taught that Prophets and Apostles were no longer needed, so some cried false Prophet. In 1831 two men preached in our settlement saying a new Prophet had organized a new church and introduced a new gospel or rather the old one come again. His name was Joseph Smith. Their names were Hyrum Smith, brother of the Prophet and John Murdock. Other Elders were passing every few months from Kirtland to Jackson County—the gathering place for the Saints, and father opened his house for meetings . . . I was baptized in Salt River on the 10th of Sept., 1832. There were 19 baptized that day including my Parents and one or two of my sisters.[52]

Isaac soon sold the family farm and moved to Jackson County, the gathering place for the new church. But when the Latter-day Saints were expelled from Jackson County, the Allreds had to find other accommodations. And that wasn't the worst of it. The prophet Joseph Smith and other leaders of the restored Church of Jesus Christ attempted to reclaim their homes and farms that had been seized by nonmembers of Jackson County. Skirmishes broke out—church militias and Missouri locals exchanged small-arms fire. Angry mobs retaliated, destroying property affiliated with the church, including the church's print shop. The Allreds and others were now refugees in their own land.

In 1835, Joseph Smith called on his followers to assemble in Clay County, Missouri, where Isaac and his family made their new home. It didn't last. Reddick's account wrote of angry locals there, too.

In 1835 father moved up to Clay and located on Fishing River where he raised one crop, and the influx was so great that the old settlers became alarmed and the mob spirit began to raise [*sic*], which was checked only by a compromise by which the old settlers were to buy out the Saints, and were to move into a new county adjoining called Caldwell County.[53]

---

[52] "Isaac Allred (27 Jan 1788–13 Nov 1870)," maintained by the Schott family (contributor 46932087), Find a Grave Memorial No. 146675, accessed September 30, 2019, www.findagrave.com/memorial/146675/isaac-allred.

[53] Ibid.

Their troubles were far from over. By 1840, local law enforcement was searching for William Allred for his involvement in armed conflicts with church settlers, so he fled the area. This left Isaac, his wife, his daughters, his youngest sons, and two ox teams (the only ones that hadn't been stolen or killed) to transport their belongings to Illinois in a wintertime exodus from Clay County.

When the Allreds reached Nauvoo, Illinois, they reunited with Joseph Smith, who'd also escaped Missouri. A few years later, the great journey westward continued. The Allred clan moved with other church members first to the Iowa side of the Mississippi River and then, finally, in October 1849, to Salt Lake City.

The Allred family had enjoyed two years of peace when Isaac's wife, Mary, passed away in September 1851. The following year, in 1852, he married Matilda Park, a widow with three children. Having already raised a family of twelve (two of whom were still teenagers), Isaac joined Matilda in raising a second family—Matilda's children, plus their new daughter. Due to unpredictable weather, life remained as hard as ever. Reddick wrote that "[the Allreds] were quite destitute having lost their crop the two successive seasons as also many others throughout the territory, especially the last season."[54]

In the spring of 1858, the Salt Lake Latter-day Saints were forced south to the Utah valley. Thus, Isaac, at age seventy-two, extended the frontier further. He remained strong and in good spirits in spite of

---

[54] Ibid.

repeated Native American and wolf attacks on his property. He kept up those good spirits until his death on November 13, 1870. He was eighty-two.

My great-grandfather and his contemporaries decided to make their journey west work. No matter what. And they did. Was it easy? Far from it. But they didn't give up. Thanks to their commitment, the western United States has gone from 268 pioneer communities in 1860 to seventy-four million people today. Family records portray my ancestor as a happy man who led a full, rich life. I know plenty of people who spend their evenings and weekends wallowing in misery, even though they experience little struggle in life. If circumstances don't control whether or not we're happy, what does?

Better Decisions, More Time, Happier Life

I believe that fulfillment comes in large part from the confidence that we're making good decisions and from a will to stick to them. You don't waste time and energy undoing choices you know you shouldn't have made. Satisfaction with your life also comes from accepting responsibility for it. Taking responsibility helps you lead a happier life and protects your precious time from poor decisions. It has an even greater influence on future generations.

Kids are always watching and always learning. It's easy for parents to step in and help their kids out. But when we do so in situations that are not dire, we steal the enjoyment kids get from figuring things out for themselves and making decisions accordingly. When our kids get to make decisions themselves, they learn what benefits them and those around them (and what doesn't). Whether you're that young adult or you already have kids, you are the product of your decisions. How will you turn out? Take some time right now. Ponder how you're going to live.

- Will you succumb to fear or stand up and be brave?

- Will you let greed drive you or will generosity lead you?

- Will pride puff you up, or will you stand down and stay humble?

- Will you wallow in shame or accept responsibility for your actions?

- Will your urges pull you into instant gratification, or will you wait for the right time and place?

- Will you count on your own experience or seek the wisdom of second opinions?

- Will you make all decisions at once or make every decision one at a time?

- Will you stay under pressure or get out and away so you can think straight?

- Will excess ruin your character or challenge you to build it?

- Will you follow through or back away?

- Will you chase trends or let the right movement move you?

- Will you surround yourself with C players, or will A players make up your team?

- Will you make an unfair situation worse or get your life back onto the fairway?

- Will you overstay your welcome or move on?

- Will you be overly optimistic about your strengths or be honest about what you do best?

- Will you put off your to-do list, or will you do those tasks right now?

- Will you make assumptions or suspend judgment until the facts come in?

- Will you give until it hurts or give until it helps?

- Will the universe revolve around you, or will you help everyone in it become self-sufficient?

  Whatever you decide, it's your choice.

  You always have a choice.

Acknowledgments

Anything good you learned from this book doesn't come from me alone but also from everyone who has touched my life. I want to thank all those whose support motivated me to write *Purify*. Thank you to the countless mentors and professionals who believe in me. Thank you also to the young men's leaders, Scout leaders, educators, and fellow members of the Church of Jesus Christ of Latter-day Saints who have shaped the person I am today. And thank you to my parents, my in-laws, my children, and my wife, Cara. Every day you all inspire me to help people throughout the earth get clean water. Thank you.

About the Author

Richard E. Allred is President, CEO, and Managing Partner of ATS. Since 1979, ATS has provided innovative solutions to protect and treat the world's water, from developing countries to businesses like Barrick Gold, Chevron, Denver Water, Phillipps 66, and Toyota. In 2010, Richard's company made headlines worldwide when ATS technology helped rescue thirty-three trapped miners in Chile. Richard also serves on the board of Empower Mali, a nonprofit that builds infrastructure to further education.

Richard was inspired to take over ATS from his father after serving a mission for the Church of Jesus Christ of Latter-day Saints to Brazil.

He realized the best way he could help people in Brazil was by providing them with clean water. Richard then expanded his charitable operations to West Africa and the Philippines. An eternal optimist, Richard believes in continual improvement both personally and professionally. Richard enjoys finding solutions to complex problems and inspiring confidence, optimism, and creativity in his employees and partners. Richard and his wife Cara live in Utah with their six children. Learn more about Richard and ATS at www.atssmartsolutions.com.

Made in the USA
San Bernardino,
CA